# PASTA
# SHMASTA

# PASTA SHMASTA

## 101 GREAT WAYS TO MAKE GOOD OLD-FASHIONED SPAGHETTI

### KAREN CROSS McKEOWN

A JOHN BOSWELL ASSOCIATES BOOK

MAIN STREET BOOKS

DOUBLEDAY
NEW YORK LONDON TORONTO SYDNEY AUCKLAND

For Caitlin

A MAIN STREET BOOK
PUBLISHED BY DOUBLEDAY

a division of Bantam Doubleday Dell Publishing Group, Inc.
1540 Broadway, New York, New York 10036

MAIN STREET BOOKS, DOUBLEDAY,
and the portrayal of a building with a tree are trademarks of Doubleday,
a division of Bantam Doubleday Dell Publishing Group, Inc.

Book Design by Barbara Cohen Aronica
Index by Maro Riofrancos

VELVEETA® is a registered trademark appearing on page 85 courtesy of Kraft General Foods, Inc.
AMERICAN BEAUTY, RONZONI, SAN GIORGIO, and SKINNER are registered trademarks.
Recipes appearing on pages 93 to 97 are courtesy of
the Hershey Kitchens, and reprinted with permission of Hershey Foods Corporation.
Recipes appearing on pages 98 to 100 are courtesy of Creamette.

Library of Congress Cataloging-in-Publication Data
McKeown, K. C.
Pasta shmasta : 101 great ways to make good
old-fashioned spaghetti / Karen Cross McKeown.
p.    cm.
"A John Boswell Associates book."
Includes index.
1. Cookery (Pasta)    I. Title.
TX809.M17M38    1995
641.8'22–dc20                     94-43982
                                              CIP

ISBN 0-385-47389-3
A John Boswell Associates Book
Printed in the United States of America
First Main Street Books Edition: April 1995

# C O N T E N T S

# INTRODUCTION

There was a time not too long ago in America's culinary past when "pasta" meant spaghetti. Whether topped with meatballs, clam sauce, or grated cheese from that familiar green canister, spaghetti (perhaps along with elbow macaroni) defined the typical American's exposure to pasta.

It was an age of culinary innocence, that time before the great pasta renaissance of the seventies and eighties; before pesto sauce became as commonly used as mayonnaise; before anyone had heard of Apulia, Istria, Lombardy, or Sardinia (let alone sampled their regional dishes) or cared about the differences between tagliolini, tagliatelle, and tagliarini.

I'm ashamed to admit it, but during those freewheeling decades when pasta in all its glorious variations was brought to the hungry masses, I too fell victim to pastamania. I sampled a veritable rainbow of strands, twists, tubes, and curlicues, from squid's ink fettuccine to saffron malloreddus to beet-flavored garganelli. I savored both Ligurian and Genoese nut sauces. I even owned a pasta machine. And *I* knew the differences between tagliolini, tagliatelle, and tagliarini!

Yet, I must also reveal a deep dark secret. During this time of ecstatic pasta devotion, I regularly bought boxes of dried spaghetti at the supermarket. Perhaps this habit of boiling up boxed spaghetti began as a reaction to what had become a question of "too much of a good thing gone bad" as far as pasta was concerned. ("Enough! Enough!" I wanted to scream every time I went to a local salad bar or diner serving some glutinous version of pasta primavera, tortellini in pesto sauce, or greasy fettuccine bolognese.) But more than that, there was something reassuring, refreshing, and deeply satisfying about such an unadorned, almost primal food that was also quick, inexpensive, and easy to make.

As far as I'm concerned, the appeal of spaghetti-in-the-box has survived the test of time and the "Me Decade" thoroughly intact. Spaghetti-in-the-box serves us well in the back-to-basics nineties, when our priorities have changed: Our lives have become more complicated, and we seem to be working harder and harder to juggle our professional and personal obligations. But that doesn't mean we have to give up all hope and settle for canned spaghetti warmed up in the microwave either.

The beauty of spaghetti from the box is its versatility and universal appeal. It's always available, all year long. It's consistent in quality. It's nutritious. It cooks in a few minutes. We all grew up eating it. We all love it, even problem eaters like children. (In fact spaghetti is so beloved around the world that no less than three distinct cultures—Chinese, Arabic, and, of course, Italian—lay claim to its invention.) Spaghetti's neutral taste is a perfect foil for every conceivable type of sauce, from slow-cooked and spicy to fresh-off-the-vine, and lickety-split. It's hard to imagine anything that would taste bad with spaghetti.

So, keeping this in mind, and at the expense of losing culinary face, I say, "Basta pasta! Pasta shmasta!" Bring on the spaghetti! Throw out the pasta machine. Forget about memorizing the names of fifty different pasta shapes! Forget about goat cheese and arugula. In *Pasta Shmasta* you'll find more than a hundred home-style, delicious, and easy-to-prepare spaghetti recipes using affordable ingredients readily available in most supermarkets and grocery stores. No white or black truffles. No $100 bottles of aged balsamic vinegar. No strong cheeses with unpronounceable names. Just honest-to-goodness, satisfying dishes.

You may be asking yourself "Well, then, what kinds of recipes *are* in this book? Spaghetti with meatballs? Spaghetti with marinara sauce?" Of course, *Pasta Shmasta* has several themes and variations on classic tomato sauces and spaghetti with meatballs. But it doesn't stop there.

The whole "pasta thing" of the previous decade did go a bit overboard. But that doesn't negate the fact that we *are* more sophisticated and knowledgeable about food and that we have been exposed to many different styles of cuisine and food preparation. We have entire cable networks devoted to cookery shows, and sales of Mexican salsa have surpassed those of ketchup. That says something about the American eating public.

With a food as versatile and tasty as spaghetti, it's simple to adapt a whole range of international flavors—Mexican, Middle Eastern, African, or Asian—to a wide variety of traditional spaghetti recipes. So, along with a master recipe for traditional spaghetti and meatballs you'll be able to find recipes for chicken meatballs in a spicy Mexican-style sauce; African-style lamb meatballs in a fruity, curry-flavored sauce; and meatballs stroganoff. Along with the standard recipe for spaghetti with garlic and olive oil, you will find international variations on simple oil and aromatic spice combinations rooted in the cuisines of Asia. You'll find hearty winter fare, cold summer dishes, and more than a few old-time classics and nostalgic favorites, almost all of the sauces designed to be cooked in a single pot in the time it takes to boil water and cook the spaghetti itself. So come on! Whether you're in the mood for good old spaghetti and meatballs, dinner in a hurry, or an exotic getaway, there's something for you in the pages of *Pasta Shmasta*.

## A NOTE ON COOKING PASTA

According to most pasta manufacturers and cookbooks, pasta should be cooked in at least 6 to 8 quarts of boiling water. However, if time is short and you're not the type who's patient enough to sit around for an eternity waiting for your water to boil, you can use about 4 quarts of water to cook 1 pound of spaghetti. Just make sure to give it a stir now and then to keep the strands from sticking together. Cook the spaghetti approximately 8 to 10 minutes for al dente, or to taste.

The debate also rages on whether to salt or not to salt (and when to salt) the cooking water for spaghetti. Adding a spoonful or two of salt to the water as it comes to the boil does produce tastier spaghetti. However, if you need to watch your sodium intake or don't like adding salt to dishes, feel free to omit it.

Try to time the cooking of the spaghetti to coincide with the completion of the sauce. However, if you need to keep the spaghetti for a short time after it's cooked, just toss it with a bit of oil, butter, or margarine to keep it from becoming a glutinous mess.

Some of the recipes in the book call for sauces or toppings that need no cooking. In these, the "Cooking Time" listed is for the spaghetti only.

# TOMATO CLASSICS

When we think of spaghetti, inevitably our minds are drawn to tomato sauces. Whether they are slowly simmered, smooth or chunky, creamy or spicy, topped with meatballs or grated cheese, there's no doubt that, for many people, this family of sauces defines the joys of eating spaghetti.

Here you'll find traditional slow-simmered sauces and several quick-cooking, one-pot versions of Italian tomato classics you can whip up in ten or fifteen minutes using a variety of fresh and canned tomatoes. Easy-to-prepare uncooked tomato sauces—aromatic combinations of juicy ripe tomatoes and fresh herbs perfect for a sultry summer day—round out the tomato repertoire.

# SPAGHETTI ALL' ARRABBIATA

*Sauce arrabbiata serves as the base for other Italian favorites: sauce Fra Diavolo and sauce puttanesca, which follow, and the red clam sauce on page 58.*

**PREP TIME:** 5 MINUTES
**COOKING TIME:** 15 MINUTES
**SERVES:** 4

3 tablespoons olive oil
2 garlic cloves, finely minced
1 (28-ounce) can Italian-style tomatoes,
    drained and coarsely chopped
1 tablespoon minced fresh parsley
½ teaspoon red pepper flakes
½ teaspoon salt
Freshly ground black pepper
1 pound dried spaghetti, cooked according to
    package directions

1. Heat the olive oil in a sauté pan over medium heat. Add the garlic and cook until golden, about 2 to 3 minutes. Be careful not to brown the garlic.

2. Add the tomatoes, parsley, red pepper, salt, and black pepper to taste. Stir until combined. Simmer over low heat for 10 minutes.

3. Serve over the cooked spaghetti.

## VARIATIONS

PUTTANESCA SAUCE: Omit the salt from the basic recipe. Add to the tomatoes 1 cup pitted black olives, ¼ cup drained capers, 4 anchovy fillets, chopped, and ½ teaspoon dried basil or 1 tablespoon chopped fresh basil. Season with salt and pepper to taste. Sprinkle with chopped parsley.

FRA DIAVOLO SAUCE: To the basic recipe add 1 tablespoon EACH chopped fresh basil, oregano, and mint (or ½ teaspoon EACH of dried) and 1 teaspoon Tabasco sauce, or to taste. Serve with grated Romano cheese.

MIXED SEAFOOD FRA DIAVOLO: Add to the cooked sauce in a single layer 12 clams, scrubbed, and 12 mussels, scrubbed and debearded. Cover and steam until they just begin to open, about 5 minutes. Add 12 large shrimp, peeled and deveined, and the meat from 2 lobster tails, sliced crosswise. Cover and steam another 5 minutes, or until cooked through.

# SPAGHETTI WITH CLASSIC ITALIAN TOMATO SAUCE

*Here's a recipe for a traditional, slow-simmered, thick and rich tomato sauce, for use as is or in combination with the recipe for spaghetti with meatballs on page 46. This is a very easy sauce that with minimum preparation pretty much takes care of itself. Cook the sauce at a bare simmer to prevent it from burning and sticking to the bottom of the pan. You should only see a few bubbles rising up through the sauce as it cooks.*

**PREP TIME:** 20 MINUTES
**COOKING TIME:** 2 TO 3 HOURS
**SERVES:** 6 TO 8

2 tablespoons olive oil
2 large celery stalks, chopped
2 large carrots, chopped
1 large onion, chopped
1 heaping tablespoon tomato paste
1 (35-ounce) can Italian-style plum tomatoes with juice
1 (35-ounce) can crushed tomatoes with juice
2 teaspoons minced garlic
2 tablespoons chopped fresh parsley
1 teaspoon salt
1 bay leaf
1 teaspoon dried oregano
1 teaspoon dried basil
2 teaspoons sugar
¼ cup full-bodied red wine
1 pound dried spaghetti, cooked according to package directions

Heat the olive oil in a 4-quart saucepan over medium heat. Sauté the celery, carrots, and onion until soft and translucent, approximately 10 minutes. Add all the remaining ingredients except the spaghetti to the pan and simmer the sauce, uncovered, at least 2 to 3 hours, preferably longer. Toss with the cooked spaghetti and serve at once.

## VARIATIONS

MARINARA SAUCE: Allow the tomato sauce to cool slightly. Process in batches in a food processor until smooth in consistency.

BOLOGNESE SAUCE: Add 1 pound ground beef to the sautéed onion, celery, and carrot. Cook beef until just slightly pink. Add 2 tablespoons vermouth and boil 2 minutes. Proceed with the recipe.

## SPAGHETTI WITH COOKED FRESH TOMATO SAUCE

*This is a dish to enjoy in summer, at the height of tomato season. The short cooking time helps retain the sweetness and freshness of the tomatoes.*

**PREP TIME:** 25 MINUTES
**COOKING TIME:** 15 MINUTES
**SERVES:** 4

2½ pounds fresh plum tomatoes
2 tablespoons sweet butter
2 tablespoons safflower or canola oil
1 medium onion, minced
1 garlic clove, minced
1 teaspoon balsamic vinegar
Salt and freshly ground black pepper
¼ cup shredded fresh basil
1 pound dried spaghetti, cooked according to
   package directions

1. Bring a few inches of water to the boil in a 4-quart saucepan. Blanch the tomatoes in the boiling water for 30 seconds. Drain and refresh with cold water. When cool enough to handle, peel, seed, and coarsely chop the tomatoes.

2. Melt the butter and oil in a 9-inch sauté pan over medium heat. Add the onion and cook until golden and translucent, about 5 minutes. Add the tomatoes, garlic, and vinegar to the pan and cook an additional 10 minutes. Season with salt and pepper to taste. Add the fresh basil and cook another 1 or 2 minutes. Serve tossed with the cooked spaghetti.

### VARIATION

SAUCE CONTADINA: Add ½ cup heavy cream and 1 tablespoon minced fresh rosemary to the sauce with the basil. Allow the sauce to cook down an additional 5 to 7 minutes, or until slightly thickened.

## SPAGHETTI AMATRICIANA

**PREP TIME:** 5 MINUTES
**COOKING TIME:** 20 MINUTES
**SERVES:** 4

2 tablespoons sweet butter
2 tablespoons vegetable oil
1 large onion, thinly sliced
1 thick slice (2 to 3 ounces) pancetta, diced
1 (28-ounce) can Italian plum tomatoes with
    their juice
1 teaspoon red pepper flakes (or to taste)
1 teaspoon salt
1 pound dried spaghetti, cooked according to
    package directions
Grated Romano cheese

1. Heat the butter and oil in a 3½-quart casserole or Dutch oven over medium heat. Add the onion and sauté until golden and translucent, about 5 minutes. Turn the heat to high. Add the pancetta and sauté 1 or 2 minutes, or until lightly browned.

2. Lower the heat and add the remaining ingredients (except for the spaghetti and cheese). Simmer 15 minutes, or until the oil begins to separate from the sauce. Toss with the cooked spaghetti and serve with the grated cheese.

## TOMATO SALSA CRUDA WITH SPAGHETTI

**PREP TIME:** 15 MINUTES
**COOKING TIME:** 10 MINUTES FOR SPAGHETTI
**SERVES:** 4

2 large tomatoes, chopped (approximately
    2 cups)
½ cup chopped jicama
2 tablespoons minced onion
1 celery stalk, minced (approximately ¼ cup)
1 tablespoon chopped fresh basil
1 teaspoon chopped fresh cilantro
¼ teaspoon ground cumin
Salt and freshly ground black pepper
1 pound dried spaghetti, cooked according to
    package directions

1. Combine the ingredients (except for spaghetti) in a small nonreactive bowl or container. Season with salt and pepper to taste.

2. Serve over the cooked spaghetti.

## SPAGHETTI WITH QUICKIE TOMATO SAUCE

*Here's a sauce you can whip up quick when you're pressed for time but still feel like having something a little bit fresher and more elegant than a jar of prepared sauce. Make sure to use tomatoes in purée, otherwise the sauce will be too thin.*

**PREP TIME:** 10 MINUTES
**COOKING TIME:** 20 MINUTES
**SERVES:** 4

3 tablespoons olive oil
1 medium onion, minced
1 (28-ounce) can Italian tomatoes in purée
1 garlic clove, minced
1 teaspoon fennel seeds
1½ tablespoons minced fresh parsley
½ teaspoon dried oregano
½ teaspoon dried basil
Salt and freshly ground black pepper
1 pound dried spaghetti, cooked according to package directions

1. Heat the oil in a 9-inch skillet or Dutch oven over medium heat. Add the onion and sauté until softened and translucent, about 5 minutes. Add all remaining ingredients except salt, pepper, and spaghetti and stir until combined.

2. Simmer over low heat for 15 to 20 minutes and season with salt and pepper to taste. Serve over cooked spaghetti.

### VARIATIONS

WOODSMAN'S SAUCE: Add to the sautéed onion 1 ounce chopped, rehydrated dried mushrooms and 1 ounce shredded prosciutto. Proceed with the recipe as above.

MEAT SAUCE: Add to the sautéed onion ¾ pound ground beef. Sauté until the beef is cooked through and no longer pink. Add remaining ingredients as above.

MUSHROOM SAUCE: Add to the sautéed onion 12 ounces sliced white mushrooms. Sauté until cooked through and proceed with the recipe.

## SPICY MEXICAN TOMATO SAUCE WITH SPAGHETTI

*This sauce can be served with spaghetti alone or with the chicken meatballs appearing on page 28.*

**PREP TIME:** 15 MINUTES
**COOKING TIME:** 30 MINUTES
**SERVES:** 4

1 tablespoon peanut oil
1 large onion, minced
1 large green bell pepper, seeded and diced
2 jalapeño peppers, seeded and thinly sliced
2 serrano peppers, seeded and thinly sliced
2 garlic cloves, minced
1 (35-ounce) can strained tomatoes
1½ tablespoons minced flat-leaf parsley
1½ tablespoons chopped fresh cilantro
½ teaspoon dried oregano, crumbled
1 teaspoon sugar
Freshly ground black pepper
Salt
1 pound dried spaghetti, cooked according to
    package directions

1. Heat the oil in a 9-inch sauté pan over medium heat. Add the onion, bell pepper, and jalapeño and serrano chiles and sauté until softened and translucent, approximately 10 minutes.

2. Add the garlic, tomatoes, parsley, cilantro, oregano, sugar, and black pepper to taste. Simmer the sauce over a very low flame for 20 minutes. Add salt to taste.

3. Serve over cooked spaghetti, with or without meatballs.

## CHERRY TOMATO AND MINT SAUCE WITH SPAGHETTI

**PREP TIME:** 15 MINUTES
**COOKING TIME:** 10 MINUTES FOR SPAGHETTI
**SERVES:** 4

2 pints cherry tomatoes, stemmed and
    washed
¼ cup olive oil
2 teaspoons freshly squeezed lemon juice
2 tablespoons minced red onion
3 tablespoons chopped fresh mint
2 small garlic cloves, minced
2 teaspoons salt
Black pepper
1 pound dried spaghetti, cooked according to
    package directions

1. Halve the cherry tomatoes and place them in a
serving dish large enough to accommodate the
spaghetti.

2. Add the remaining ingredients (except
spaghetti) to the tomatoes and combine thoroughly.
Toss together with the cooked spaghetti and serve
immediately.

## SPAGHETTI WITH SUN-DRIED TOMATO SAUCE

**PREP TIME:** 30 MINUTES
**COOKING TIME:** 10 MINUTES FOR SPAGHETTI
**SERVES:** 4

4 ounces sun-dried tomatoes
¼ cup olive oil
2 teaspoons minced garlic
3 tablespoons toasted pine nuts
¼ cup shredded fresh basil leaves
4 ounces mozzarella cheese, cut into ½-inch
    cubes
Salt and freshly ground black pepper
1 pound dried spaghetti, cooked according to
    package directions

1. Place the tomatoes in a heatproof bowl. Cover
with boiling water and leave until softened,
approximately 30 minutes. Drain thoroughly;
coarsely chop.

2. Add the olive oil, garlic, pine nuts, basil, and
mozzarella cheese to the tomatoes and toss to
combine. Season with salt and pepper to taste. Toss
with the cooked spaghetti and serve immediately.

# A CORNUCOPIA OF VEGETABLES

Every year we await the first pencil-thin asparagus of spring, relish the bounty of summer squash and tomatoes, and sadly say good-bye to the last sweet corn of September.

The toppings appearing in this chapter showcase these vegetables and more in all their glory. Most are best savored in season. But because—thanks to the global marketplace—a wider variety of products is now available year-round, you might well be able to satisfy a bad hankering for fresh basil or summer squash in the dead of February.

The recipes are quite straightforward and easy to prepare, but do require a bit of advance work in terms of peeling, seeding, chopping, and dicing the vegetables. With the exception of just a few, the recipes are entirely vegetarian as well. If you do not wish to use meat products or stock in a particular dish, substitute an appropriate vegetable broth or oil instead.

# SPAGHETTI WITH ASPARAGUS, SWEET ONION, AND GORGONZOLA

**PREP TIME:** 10 MINUTES
**COOKING TIME:** 15 MINUTES
**SERVES:** 4

1 pound fresh asparagus, cut into 2-inch
    pieces
2 tablespoons sweet butter
2 tablespoons safflower or canola oil
1 Vidalia or other sweet onion (about
    ⅓ pound), sliced very thin
1 tablespoon dry sherry
2 ounces Gorgonzola cheese (dolce or picante,
    as desired)
Salt
1 pound dried spaghetti, cooked according to
    package directions

1. In a 9-inch sauté pan, bring an inch of salted water to a boil. Drop the asparagus into the boiling water and cook until crisp-tender, about 3 to 5 minutes. Drain and refresh in cold water.

2. Dry the pan thoroughly and in it melt the butter and oil over medium heat. Add the onion and sauté until soft and translucent, approximately 5 minutes. Add the sherry and cook another minute. Add the Gorgonzola and stir until melted. Stir in the asparagus. Salt to taste.

3. Drain the spaghetti and toss with the onion-asparagus mixture. Serve immediately.

## SPAGHETTI WITH BEETS AND SOUR CREAM

*This recipe, borrowing from Scandinavian and Eastern European influences, is easy to make and will turn your spaghetti the most extraordinary shocking-pink color. If you have the time, use fresh beets, which have an earthier, sweeter flavor than canned. Substitute about 4 cups diced canned beets in a pinch.*

**PREP TIME:** 10 MINUTES
**COOKING TIME:** 1 HOUR
**SERVES:** 4

1½ pounds fresh beets, scrubbed clean
½ cup beef broth
1½ teaspoons prepared Dijon mustard
½ cup sour cream
1 tablespoon snipped fresh dill weed
1 pound dried spaghetti, cooked according to
    package directions
1 hard-cooked egg, chopped (optional
    garnish)

1. Place the beets in a saucepan with enough water to cover them completely. Simmer, partially covered, until they are tender, about an hour (the time will vary depending upon the size of the beets). When they are cool enough to handle, peel the beets and cut them into ½-inch dice.

2. While the beets are cooking, combine the beef broth, mustard, and sour cream in a saucepan over medium heat. Stir until thoroughly mixed. Add the beets and toss until coated and heated through. Add the dill weed and serve immediately over the cooked spaghetti, sprinkling the chopped egg over the top if you like.

## SPAGHETTI WITH BROCCOLI RABE AND WHITE BEANS

**PREP TIME:** 10 MINUTES
**COOKING TIME:** 10 MINUTES
**SERVES:** 4

1¾ pounds (approximately 2 bunches)
    broccoli rabe, tough stems removed
½ cup good-quality olive oil
1½ teaspoons salt
6 garlic cloves, thinly sliced (more or less, to
    taste)
1½ teaspoons salt
1 cup cooked white beans
2 tablespoons dry white wine
1 pound dried spaghetti, cooked according to
    package directions

1. While the spaghetti is cooking, blanch the broccoli rabe in 1 inch of salted boiling water and cook until it is wilted, about 3 to 4 minutes. Drain the broccoli rabe and refresh it with cold water. When it is cool enough to handle, squeeze out any excess water and coarsely chop.

2. Heat the olive oil in a 9-inch sauté pan over medium-high heat. Add the salt and garlic to the hot oil and cook until the garlic is lightly browned, being careful not to burn it.

3. Add the broccoli rabe and the white beans to the browned garlic and oil and cook until heated through. Lower the heat and add the wine. Cook for 1 or 2 minutes longer. Toss with the hot spaghetti and serve immediately

# CAULIFLOWER IN BROWN BUTTER WITH HAZELNUTS

*Cauliflower in brown or browned butter sauce is an inexpensive yet elegant dish, and a breeze to prepare. However, beware: There is a very thin line between browned butter and burnt butter. So, when you melt the butter, do it over heat high enough to cause the butter to bubble and cook, but not so high that the milk solids in the butter scorch and stick to the pan. Try to use the freshest, sweetest butter you can find to achieve the best flavor possible.*

**PREP TIME:** 15 MINUTES
**COOKING TIME:** 20 MINUTES
**SERVES:** 4

¼ **cup milk**
**2 small heads cauliflower, broken into bite-sized florets (about 6 cups)**
½ **pound (2 sticks) sweet butter, cut up**
**1 pound dried spaghetti, cooked according to package directions**
**2 tablespoons minced fresh parsley**
**Salt**
**2 ounces hazelnuts, toasted and chopped***

1. In a 4-quart saucepan or Dutch oven, bring to a boil the milk and enough salted water to cover the cauliflower. Drop the cauliflower into the boiling water and cook the florets until crisp-tender, about 3 to 5 minutes. Drain and refresh in cold water. (You can do this a day ahead and refrigerate the florets. Bring back to room temperature before proceeding with the recipe.)

2. A few minutes before you are ready to drop the spaghetti into boiling water, melt the butter over medium heat in the dry 4-quart saucepan. Stir occasionally and continue cooking until the butter begins to turn golden brown, about 12 to 15 minutes. Watch the butter carefully as it cooks. Remove from the heat and toss with the cauliflower.

3. Place the cooked spaghetti in a large warm serving dish and toss it with the browned butter, cauliflower, and parsley until thoroughly combined. Season with salt to taste. Top with the chopped hazelnuts. Serve immediately.

* To toast hazelnuts: Place the nuts in a single layer on a pan in a 350 degree oven for about 10 minutes, or until their skins begin to peel. Rub the hazelnuts together in a clean dish towel to remove the skins.

## SPAGHETTI WITH CREAMY CORN AND POBLANO CHILES

**PREP TIME:** 25 MINUTES
**COOKING TIME:** 15 MINUTES
**SERVES:** 4

4 poblano chiles
1 tablespoon safflower or canola oil
2 tablespoons sweet butter
1 medium onion, minced
3 cups corn kernels, preferably fresh
1 garlic clove, minced
¼ teaspoon dried thyme
1 cup grated Jack cheese
½ cup sour cream
1 tablespoon chopped fresh cilantro
Salt and freshly ground black pepper
1 pound spaghetti, cooked according to
    package directions

1. Preheat the broiler.

2. Place the poblano chiles under the broiler, turning occasionally, until the skin is blackened and blistered all over. Place the chiles in a brown paper bag for 5 minutes to steam. Peel the chiles, remove the stems, seeds, and membranes, and cut the chile flesh into strips. Toss with the oil and set aside. (You can do this much a day ahead and refrigerate the chile strips.)

3. Heat the butter in a 9-inch sauté pan over medium heat. Add the onion and sauté until softened and translucent, about 5 minutes. Add the corn, garlic, and thyme and sauté until cooked through, 7 to 8 minutes for fresh corn, 1 to 2 minutes for canned.

4. Add the cheese, sour cream, and cilantro to the corn. Toss in the chile strips and season with salt and pepper to taste. Serve immediately over the cooked spaghetti.

## SPAGHETTI WITH GREEN BEANS AND BACON

**PREP TIME:** 15 MINUTES
**COOKING TIME:** 15 MINUTES
**SERVES:** 4

1¼ pounds green beans, trimmed and cut into
    2-inch pieces
6 ounces thick-cut bacon, cut into ¼ x 1-inch
    lardons
Vegetable oil (if necessary)
1 small onion, thinly sliced
1 pound dried spaghetti, cooked according to
    package directions
Grated Parmesan cheese

1. In a 2-quart saucepan, bring to a boil approximately 1 inch of salted water. Drop the green beans into the water and cook until tender to the bite. Drain, refresh with cold water, and set aside.

2. Place the bacon in a 9-inch sauté pan over medium heat and cook until it begins to render its fat. (The thicker the bacon, the less fat it seems to render. If the pan is quite dry, add a tablespoon or so of oil to help the process along.) Add the onion and sauté until it is golden and translucent, approximately 5 minutes. Add the cooked green beans and toss until heated through.

3. Serve immediately over spaghetti and top with grated Parmesan, if desired.

## SPAGHETTI WITH MIXED VEGETABLES IN ORANGE BUTTER SAUCE

**PREP TIME:** 20 MINUTES
**COOKING TIME:** 15 MINUTES
**SERVES:** 4

½ small head cauliflower (approximately 2 cups florets)
Salt
2 large carrots (approximately 2 cups), thinly sliced on the diagonal
2 cups snow peas
4 tablespoons (½ stick) sweet butter
1 teaspoon arrowroot
¼ cup chicken broth
2 tablespoons freshly squeezed orange juice
1 teaspoon grated orange zest
1 small garlic clove, minced
2 tablespoons dry white wine
2 tablespoons snipped fresh chives
1 pound dried spaghetti, cooked according to package directions

1. Boil approximately 2 cups salted water in a 2-quart saucepan. Drop the cauliflower into the water and cook until tender, 2 or 3 minutes. Remove the cauliflower from the water with a metal strainer or slotted spoon. Refresh with cold water. Next, cook the carrot slices in the boiling water until they are tender, approximately 3 to 4 minutes Remove the carrots with a slotted spoon and refresh with cold water. Drop the snow peas in the water. Cook until tender and bright green, about 1 or 2 minutes. Drain and refresh with cold water.

2. In a 9-inch sauté pan, melt the butter over medium heat. Dissolve the arrowroot in a bit of the chicken broth. Add to the butter the remaining chicken broth, the orange juice, orange zest, garlic, white wine, and arrowroot mixture. Whisk until combined and slightly thickened. Season with salt to taste.

3. Add the vegetables to the butter sauce and toss until heated through. Add the chives and serve immediately over the cooked spaghetti.

# SPAGHETTI WITH SUMMER VEGETABLE MEDLEY

*Every home gardener, while reveling in the bounty of summer's vegetable harvest, may be equally perplexed at how to dispose of all these glorious vegetables. Here's the perfect solution! This vegetable stew, a version of the famous French ratatouille, is a perfect way to use all your home-grown tomatoes, eggplants, zucchini, and peppers. It's delicious on spaghetti, in omelets, or as a side dish. The taste improves with a couple of days' refrigeration, and you can freeze it too.*

**PREP TIME:** 25 MINUTES
**COOKING TIME:** 1 HOUR
**SERVES:** 6

¼ cup olive oil
1 large onion, cubed
1 large green bell pepper (about ½ pound), seeded and cubed
1 large red bell pepper (about ½ pound), seeded and cubed
1 eggplant (about 1¼ pounds), cut into 1-inch cubes
1¼ pounds zucchini, cut into 1-inch-thick slices
2 cups peeled, seeded, drained, chopped fresh tomatoes OR 1 cup puréed tomatoes
2 garlic cloves, minced
2 teaspoons fresh thyme OR 1 teaspoon dried thyme
2 teaspoons fresh oregano OR 1 teaspoon dried oregano
1 tablespoon fresh basil leaf OR ½ teaspoon dried basil
1 tablespoon minced fresh parsley
Salt and pepper
1½ pounds dried spaghetti, cooked according to package directions

1. Heat the oil in a 3-quart Dutch oven over medium heat. Add the onion and the green and red peppers and sauté until the onion is softened and translucent, about 7 or 8 minutes. Turn the heat up slightly and add the eggplant and zucchini. Toss until lightly browned.

2. Lower the heat and add the tomatoes, garlic, and herbs. Simmer, partially covered, stirring occasionally, for 45 minutes, or until all the vegetables are tender and cooked through. Season with salt and pepper to taste. Serve over the cooked spaghetti.

## SPAGHETTI WITH VEGETARIAN CHILI

*Don't let the long list of ingredients intimidate you. This is a breeze to prepare and if you have leftover sauce, it can be frozen.*

**PREP TIME:** 30 MINUTES
**COOKING TIME:** 30 MINUTES
**SERVES:** 6 TO 8

2 tablespoons safflower or canola oil
1 large onion, minced
1 celery stalk, minced
1 large carrot, diced (about 1 cup)
½ large green bell pepper, seeded and diced (about ½ cup)
½ large red bell pepper, seeded and diced (about ½ cup)
2 jalapeño peppers, seeded and sliced
1 large zucchini, diced (about 1 cup)
1 large yellow summer squash, diced (about 1 cup)
2 teaspoons minced garlic
2 teaspoons ground red pepper
2 teaspoons ground cumin
½ teaspoon cayenne pepper

2 bay leaves
1 teaspoon dried oregano, crumbled
1 cup tomato purée OR 2 cups chopped fresh peeled and seeded tomatoes
1 cup water (only if using tomato purée)
½ cup corn kernels
1 cup cooked black beans
1 cup cooked red kidney beans
Salt and freshly ground black pepper
1½ pounds dried spaghetti, cooked according to package directions

1. Heat the oil in a 3½-quart casserole over medium heat. Add the onion, celery, and carrot and sauté until softened, about 10 minutes. Add the green and red bell peppers and the jalapeños and sauté another few minutes until the peppers are slightly softened.

2. Add the zucchini, yellow squash, garlic, spices, herbs, and tomatoes (and water, if using tomato purée). Lower the heat and simmer, uncovered, for approximately 20 minutes, or until all vegetables are cooked through but still retain some crispness.

3. Add the corn, black beans and kidney beans, and salt and pepper to taste. Toss with the spaghetti and serve at once.

# SPAGHETTI WITH WILD MUSHROOMS

*There's nothing quite like that earthy, deep flavor of wild mushrooms. This is a perfect dish for autumn, when wild mushrooms are widely available. While this recipe calls for a combination of cultivated, oyster, and shiitake mushrooms, you can use any type of wild mushrooms you wish—morels, chanterelles, trumpet mushrooms, or others. It would also be lovely with some sautéed chicken or stewed veal mixed in.*

**PREP TIME:** 15 MINUTES
**COOKING TIME:** 15 MINUTES
**SERVES:** 4

5 tablespoons sweet butter
2 large shallots, minced
10 ounces white mushrooms, stemmed and
    sliced
5 ounces fresh shiitakes, stemmed and
    quartered
5 ounces fresh oyster mushrooms. stemmed
    and cut up
1 large garlic clove, minced
1½ teaspoons minced fresh rosemary or
    thyme

½ cup light cream
Salt and pepper
1 pound dried spaghetti, cooked according to
    package directions
Grated Parmesan cheese

1. Heat the butter in a 9-inch sauté pan over medium heat. Add the shallots and sauté until softened and translucent, about 2 to 3 minutes. Add the mushrooms, garlic, and rosemary and sauté, stirring occasionally, until the mushrooms are cooked through, about 8 to 10 minutes.

2. Add the cream and season with salt and pepper to taste. Serve with the spaghetti and sprinkle with grated Parmesan.

## SPAGHETTI WITH SPINACH AND FETA CHEESE

**PREP TIME:** 25 MINUTES
**COOKING TIME:** 10 MINUTES
**SERVES:** 4

2 pounds fresh spinach, stemmed and washed
2 tablespoons olive oil
1 small onion, minced
1 garlic clove, minced
¼ cup pine nuts
⅓ pound feta cheese, crumbled (at room
   temperature)
1 cup ricotta cheese (at room temperature)
¼ cup snipped dill weed
Salt and pepper
1 pound dried spaghetti, cooked according to
   package directions

1. Place the spinach, with the water clinging to its leaves, in a 4-quart saucepan over medium heat. Cook the spinach briefly until it wilts. Drain and refresh with cold water. When cool enough to handle, squeeze all excess water from the spinach and chop fine.

2. Heat the oil in a 9-inch sauté pan over medium heat. Add the onion and cook until golden and translucent, about 5 minutes. Add the garlic and pine nuts to the onion and cook, stirring, until the pine nuts begin to brown. Add the spinach and cook until heated through. Remove from the heat.

3. In a warm serving dish large enough to hold the spaghetti, combine the spinach, onion mixture, feta, ricotta, dill weed, and salt and pepper to taste. Mix thoroughly and toss with the hot spaghetti. Serve immediately.

## SPAGHETTI WITH WINTER VEGETABLES

**PREP TIME:** 20 MINUTES
**COOKING TIME:** 20 MINUTES
**SERVES:** 4

¾ pound (2 large) carrots, cut into ¼-inch
    dice
¾ pound rutabaga (yellow turnip), peeled and
    cut into ¼-inch dice
Salt
3 tablespoons sweet butter
1 large leek (the white and about an inch of
    green), thinly sliced
⅓ pound baked ham or ham steak, cubed
¼ cup beef broth
½ cup light cream
Salt
1 pound dried spaghetti, cooked according to
    package directions
Grated Parmesan cheese

1.  Place the carrots and rutabaga in a 2-quart saucepan with enough salted water to cover them. Bring to a boil and cook until tender, approximately 7 to 8 minutes. Drain and set aside.

2.  While the carrots and rutabaga are cooking, melt the butter in a 9-inch sauté pan over medium heat. Add the leek and sauté until golden and translucent, approximately 7 minutes. Add the ham and sauté until heated through.

3.  Add the carrots, rutabaga, beef broth, and cream to the pan. Cook over medium heat until heated through and slightly thickened. Season with salt to taste. Serve immediately over cooked spaghetti. Top with grated Parmesan cheese.

## SPAGHETTI WITH ZUCCHINI AND LEEK

*When using leeks, always be sure to quarter them lengthwise and wash all dirt or sand from between their roots and leaves.*

**PREP TIME:** 15 MINUTES
**COOKING TIME:** 10 MINUTES
**SERVES:** 4

Salt
4 medium (1½ pounds) zucchini, trimmed
  and thinly sliced
3 tablespoons sweet butter
1 large leek (the white and an inch of green),
  thinly sliced
1 tablespoon flour
¼ cup dry white wine
¼ cup chicken broth
½ teaspoon minced garlic
Freshly ground black pepper
1 pound dried spaghetti, cooked according to
  package directions

1. In a 2-quart saucepan, bring to the boil enough salted water to cover the zucchini. Drop the zucchini into the water and cook until crisp-tender, approximately 1 or 2 minutes. Drain and refresh with cold water.

2. Melt the butter in a 9-inch sauté pan over medium heat. Add the sliced leek and sauté until golden and translucent, approximately 7 minutes. Add the flour, stirring to incorporate it thoroughly. Cook another 2 minutes.

3. Add the wine, chicken broth, and garlic to the leek mixture, stirring to make a lightly thickened sauce. Season with salt and pepper to taste. Add the zucchini and toss until thoroughly combined and heated through.

4. Serve immediately over the cooked spaghetti.

# FOWL PLAY

This chapter showcases a wide range of international and ethnic flavor combinations paired primarily with chicken, but also with turkey and duck. I've used skinless, boneless, cut-up poultry or ground poultry (white meat whenever feasible) in all the recipes because they cook quickly, make a neater presentation, and are easier to eat as a topping with spaghetti. And for the health-conscious, they are a lower-fat alternative to dark meat and chicken on the bone.

# SPAGHETTI WITH CAJUN CHICKEN SAUCE

**PREP TIME:** 15 MINUTES
**COOKING TIME:** 15 MINUTES
**SERVES:** 4

2 tablespoons safflower or canola oil
1 large onion, minced
2 large celery stalks, minced
1 large green bell pepper, seeded and diced
1¼ pounds ground chicken
2 teaspoons Cajun Spice mixture* (more or
    less, to taste)
1 cup chopped canned tomatoes, drained
1 pound dried spaghetti, cooked according to
    package directions

1. Heat the oil in a 9-inch sauté pan or casserole over medium heat. Add the onion, celery, and green pepper and sauté until softened and translucent, about 10 minutes

2. Add the chicken to the vegetable mixture and break it up into small bits with a spatula. Add the Cajun Spice and sauté until the chicken is cooked through, approximately 5 minutes. Add the tomatoes and cook until heated through. Serve over the spaghetti.

* Cajun Spice mixture: In a small bowl, combine 1 tablespoon coarse or kosher salt; 1½ teaspoons sweet paprika; 1 teaspoon EACH black pepper, cayenne pepper, white pepper, dried oregano, and dried thyme; ½ teaspoon EACH onion and garlic powder.

## SPAGHETTI WITH FENNEL CHICKEN

**PREP TIME:** 15 MINUTES
**COOKING TIME:** 50 MINUTES
**SERVES:** 4

1½ pounds boneless, skinless chicken breasts
(4 breast halves)
Flour, seasoned with salt and pepper (for
dredging the chicken)
2 tablespoons safflower or canola oil
1 large onion, thinly sliced
1 fennel bulb (about 1½ pounds), trimmed
and thinly sliced
3 (½ x 3-inch) slices orange rind
Juice of 1 large orange
¼ cup white wine vinegar
2 cups canned tomatoes, with their juice
1 garlic clove, minced
Freshly ground black pepper
1 pound dried spaghetti, cooked according to
package directions

1. Cut the chicken breasts in half lengthwise and then twice more across to make 6 small chunks. Dredge the chicken pieces in the flour mixture, shaking off any excess.

2. Heat the oil over medium-high heat in a 3-quart casserole. Place the chicken pieces in the hot oil, in batches if necessary to avoid crowding, and brown on all sides. Remove the chicken pieces and set aside.

3. Lower the heat slightly. Place the onion and fennel in the casserole and sauté, scraping up any browned bits on the bottom of the pan. Cook until soft and translucent, about 10 to 15 minutes. Add the chicken and the remaining ingredients (except spaghetti). Lower the heat and simmer, partially covered, for ½ hour, or until the chicken is cooked through. (The sauce can be prepared a day or two ahead, refrigerated, and reheated.)

4. While the water for the spaghetti is boiling, remove the chicken pieces from the sauce. Purée the sauce in a food mill or in a blender or food processor. Serve the sauce over the hot spaghetti, topped with the chicken.

## SPAGHETTI WITH CHICKEN GUMBO SAUCE

**PREP TIME:** 20 MINUTES
**COOKING TIME:** 1 HOUR
**SERVES:** 4

2 tablespoons safflower or canola oil
4 boneless, skinless chicken breast halves,
    cut into 1-inch pieces
1 medium onion, chopped
2 celery stalks, chopped
1 medium green bell pepper, seeded and
    chopped
1 tablespoon filé powder*
1½ teaspoons Cajun Spice mixture (page 24)
1½ cups chicken broth
1 bay leaf
1 garlic clove, minced
2 cups sliced okra
½ tablespoon tomato paste
1 cup canned plum tomatoes, drained
Tabasco sauce
1 pound dried spaghetti, cooked according to
    package directions

1. Heat the oil over medium-high heat in a 2½- or 3½-quart casserole. Add the chicken pieces, in batches if necessary to prevent crowding, and cook until browned on all sides. Remove the chicken with a slotted spoon and set aside.

2. Add the onion, celery, and green pepper to the casserole and cook until softened and translucent, about 8 to 10 minutes. Add the filé powder and Cajun Spice to the vegetables, stirring constantly for 2 or 3 minutes.

3. Lower the heat, return the chicken to the pan, and add all remaining ingredients (except spaghetti). Simmer, covered, over low heat for 30 minutes, or until the chicken is cooked through. Serve with the cooked spaghetti.

* Filé powder is a pungent thickener made from the ground leaves of the sassafras tree.

### VARIATIONS

SHRIMP AND SAUSAGE GUMBO: Substitute 1 pound peeled shrimp and ½ pound andouille sausage for the chicken. Sauté the sausage in the oil and set aside. Sauté the shrimp until cooked through and set aside. After sautéing the vegetables, filé, and Cajun Spice, add the sausage and remaining ingredients to the casserole, but do not add the shrimp until the last 5 minutes of cooking. You just want to heat them through, not overcook them.

CHICKEN AND SAUSAGE GUMBO: Add ½ pound andouille sausage to the basic recipe, brown with the chicken, and return to the pan with the chicken as instructed in Step 3.

# SPAGHETTI WITH TARRAGON CHICKEN

**PREP TIME:** 10 MINUTES
**COOKING TIME:** 20 MINUTES
**SERVES:** 4

4 boneless, skinless chicken breast halves
¾ cup mayonnaise
2 or 3 garlic cloves, finely minced
2 tablespoons olive oil
1½ tablespoons minced fresh tarragon
Salt and pepper
1 cup cooked peas
1 pound dried spaghetti, cooked according to
    package directions

1. Preheat the oven to 350 degrees.

2. Cut each chicken breast half into 3 or 4 lengthwise slices. Cut these in thirds crosswise.

3. In a small flat nonreactive baking dish, combine the mayonnaise, garlic, olive oil, and tarragon. Season with salt and pepper to taste. Toss with the chicken pieces to coat thoroughly. Bake, covered, for 15 minutes, then uncover and bake an additional 5 minutes. Toss with the peas and cooked spaghetti. Serve immediately.

## SPAGHETTI WITH CHICKEN MEATBALLS IN SPICY MEXICAN TOMATO SAUCE

*The meatballs in this recipe, made from delicately spiced ground chicken, are quite low in fat because they are poached in hot water rather than sautéed. They have a light, fluffy texture and retain a lovely pure white color that is striking against the chunky red and green sauce spiced up with jalapeño and serrano peppers.*

**PREP TIME:** 25 MINUTES
**COOKING TIME:** 10 MINUTES
**SERVES:** 4

4 slices white bread (crusts removed ) soaked
    in ⅓ cup milk
1 pound ground white meat of chicken
1 extra large egg white
2 tablespoons minced onion
1 teaspoon minced garlic
¼ teaspoon EACH ground cumin and ground
    coriander
1 teaspoon chopped fresh cilantro
Salt and white pepper
Spicy Mexican Tomato Sauce (page 7)

1 pound dried spaghetti, cooked according to
    package directions

1. To the softened bread and milk mixture, add the chicken, egg white, onion, garlic, cumin, coriander, cilantro, and salt and white pepper to taste. (To taste for seasoning, fry a small bit of the mixture in a sauté pan over medium heat until cooked through.) Stir with a fork until all ingredients are thoroughly combined. Refrigerate the meat mixture for 15 to 20 minutes.

2. Bring an inch of water to a boil in a 9-inch sauté pan. While the water is coming to a boil, shape the meat mixture into 16 meatballs using a ⅛-cup measure. (The mixture will be quite sticky and the meatballs slightly irregular in shape.) Place the meatballs on a heatproof plate. To loosen the meatballs from the plate, ladle a bit of the boiling water over them. The meatballs will slip into the water.

3. Lower the heat and simmer the meatballs, covered, over low heat for 8 to 10 minutes, or until thoroughly cooked. (These can be prepared a day ahead, refrigerated, and reheated in the sauce.)

4. When ready to serve, combine meatballs with sauce and pour over cooked spaghetti.

## SPAGHETTI WITH NEW MEXICAN CHICKEN SAUCE

*Buy prepared New Mexican chili paste made from dried chile pods, if locally available, to cut down on the preparation time.*

**PREP TIME:** 10 MINUTES
**COOKING TIME:** 30 TO 40 MINUTES
**SERVES:** 4

2 tablespoons peanut oil
¼ cup minced onion
1½ pounds boneless, skinless chicken breasts
 (4 breast halves) each cut into 6 pieces
2 garlic cloves, minced
1 cup New Mexican chili paste*
4 (2-inch) slices orange peel
2 (2-inch) slices lemon peel
¼ cup freshly squeezed orange juice
2 tablespoons cider vinegar
1½ teaspoons salt
1 teaspoon oregano leaves
1 teaspoon ground cumin
¼ teaspoon ground cinnamon
⅛ teaspoon ground cloves
Juice of 1 lime

2 tablespoons tomato paste
2 teaspoons granulated sugar
1½ cups water
1 pound dried spaghetti, cooked according to
 package directions

1. Heat the oil in a 3½-quart Dutch oven over medium heat. Add the onion and sauté until golden, about 3 to 5 minutes. Add the chicken pieces and sauté until lightly browned on all sides.

2. Add the remaining ingredients (except spaghetti) and stir to combine thoroughly. Bring the mixture to a boil. Lower the heat and simmer, uncovered, for 30 minutes, or until chicken is cooked through and no longer pink.

3. Serve over the cooked spaghetti.

* Add an extra 45 minutes of preparation time if using dried chile pods. To rehydrate dried chiles, rinse, stem, and seed 24 dried chile pods and place them in a bowl with enough hot water to cover completely. Let the chiles soak for half an hour, or until they are softened. Remove the chiles from the water. With a butter knife or spoon, scrape out the pulp from each chile, discarding the skin and any tough membranes.

# CHICKEN PAPRIKASH AND SPAGHETTI

**PREP TIME:** 10 MINUTES
**COOKING TIME:** 50 MINUTES
**SERVES:** 4

1½ pounds boneless, skinless chicken breasts
    (4 breast halves)
Flour, seasoned with salt and pepper (for
    dredging the chicken)
2 tablespoons safflower or canola oil
1 large onion, minced
1 large carrot, diced
1 tablespoon paprika
1 cup chicken broth
½ cup dry white wine
1 cup chopped canned tomatoes, with their
    juice
1 garlic clove, minced
½ cup sour cream
Salt and freshly ground black pepper
1 pound dried spaghetti, cooked according to
    package directions

1. Cut the chicken breasts in half lengthwise and then twice more across to make 6 small chunks. Dredge the pieces in the flour and shake off any excess.

2. Heat the oil in a 3½-quart casserole over medium-high heat. Add the chicken pieces to the hot oil, in batches if necessary to prevent crowding, and sauté them until golden brown on all sides. Remove the chicken pieces with a slotted spoon.

3. Lower the heat slightly and add the onion and carrot to the casserole, stirring to scrape up any browned bits from the bottom of the pan. Sauté until softened, about 10 minutes. Add the paprika, stirring constantly for a minute or two. Return the chicken to the pan, along with the chicken broth, wine, tomatoes, and garlic. Lower heat and simmer the chicken, partially covered, for ½ hour, or until cooked through. (This can be prepared up to 2 days ahead of time and reheated.)

4. Before serving, stir the ½ cup of sour cream into the reheated sauce and heat gently for a few seconds. Season with salt and pepper to taste. Serve with the cooked spaghetti.

## SPAGHETTI WITH CHICKEN AND "POT PIE" VEGETABLES

*You may substitute thawed frozen peas for fresh. If using the frozen peas, add them to the chicken along with the cream at the end of the cooking time.*

**PREP TIME:** 15 MINUTES
**COOKING TIME:** 15 MINUTES
**SERVES:** 4

1 large carrot, diced
Salt
2 tablespoons sweet butter
1 small onion, minced
2 stalks celery, thinly sliced on the diagonal
¾ pound boneless, skinless chicken breasts
    (2 breast halves), cut into ½-inch cubes
½ cup shelled fresh or thawed frozen peas
1½ teaspoons EACH fresh thyme and tarragon
    OR ½ teaspoon EACH dried
1 small bay leaf
½ cup chicken stock
¼ cup light cream
White pepper
1 pound dried spaghetti, cooked according to
    package directions

1. Place the carrot in a small saucepan with enough salted water to cover. Bring to a boil and cook until tender, approximately 5 to 6 minutes. Drain well.

2. While the carrot is cooking, melt the butter in a 9-inch sauté pan or skillet over medium heat. Add the onion and celery and sauté until softened and translucent, approximately 5 to 7 minutes. Turn the heat up slightly and add the chicken cubes. Stir until lightly browned. Lower the heat and add the carrots, peas, herbs, and chicken stock. Cook 7 or 8 minutes, or until the chicken is no longer pink inside. Add the cream and salt and pepper to taste. Serve over the cooked spaghetti.

# SPAGHETTI AND ROSEMARY CHICKEN

**PREP TIME:** 5 MINUTES
**COOKING TIME:** 30 MINUTES
**SERVES:** 4

2 tablespoons olive oil
4 boneless, skinless chicken breast halves,
    cut into 6 pieces
1 onion, minced
2 garlic cloves, minced
1 cup chicken broth
1 large sprig fresh rosemary
Salt and pepper
1 pound dried spaghetti, cooked according to
    package directions

1. Heat the oil in a 2- or 3-quart casserole or Dutch oven. Add the chicken pieces, in batches if necessary to prevent crowding, and brown on all sides. Remove the chicken pieces with a slotted spoon and set aside.

2. Add the onion and garlic to the casserole and sauté until golden and translucent, about 5 minutes. Add the chicken and remaining ingredients (except spaghetti) and simmer, partially covered, 20 minutes, or until chicken is cooked through. Remove the rosemary sprig.

3. Serve with the cooked spaghetti.

## VARIATION

CHICKEN SCARPARIELLO: Along with the onion, brown ½ pound sweet Italian sausages, cut into ½-inch slices.

## SPAGHETTI AND CHICKEN LIVERS WITH SAGE

*If you prefer a lighter, more delicate taste, substitute sweet butter for the olive oil. You can also use fresh rosemary instead of the sage, or a combination of the two.*

**PREP TIME:** 10 MINUTES
**COOKING TIME:** 20 MINUTES
**SERVES:** 4

3 tablespoons olive oil
1 small onion, minced
1 pound chicken livers, trimmed and halved
1 teaspoon minced garlic
1 cup chopped tomatoes, preferably fresh
1 tablespoon minced fresh sage OR 1 teaspoon
    dried sage
1 pound dried spaghetti, cooked according to
    package directions

1. Heat the oil in a 9-inch sauté pan over medium heat. Add the onion and sauté until golden and translucent, about 5 minutes. Turn the heat up slightly and add the chicken livers. Sauté, tossing or stirring frequently to prevent sticking, until the chicken livers are nicely browned, about 5 minutes longer.

2. Lower the heat and add the garlic, tomatoes, and sage. Simmer another 10 minutes, or until the tomatoes are cooked through. Serve immediately with the cooked spaghetti.

# SPAGHETTI WITH DUCK AND FIGS

*If you want a devastatingly rich garnish for this dish, you can make cracklings from the skin. Just chop the skin into small pieces. Place them in a saucepan and cook until the fat is rendered and the skin is golden. Discard the fat and sprinkle the cracklings over the finished dish just before serving.*

**PREP TIME:** 15 MINUTES
**COOKING TIME:** 20 MINUTES
**SERVES:** 4

2 tablespoons sweet butter
1 whole boneless duck breast (about 2
    pounds), skinned and cut into ¼-inch-
    thick slices
1 large shallot, minced
1½ tablespoons red fruit vinegar (for example,
    raspberry or blueberry)
⅜ cup dry red wine
½ cup orange juice
Grated zest of orange
2 tablespoons honey
¾ cup chicken or duck stock
4 whole cloves

1½ teaspoons arrowroot
Salt and freshly ground black pepper
8 dried figs, quartered and soaked in 2
    tablespoons orange brandy
1 pound dried spaghetti, cooked according to
    package directions

1. Heat the butter in a large sauté pan over medium-high heat. Add the duck slices, in batches if necessary to prevent crowding, and sauté until browned on both sides, about 2 to 3 minutes total. Remove the duck with a slotted spoon and set aside.

2. Add the shallot to the pan and sauté until golden, about 2 or 3 minutes. Add the vinegar, red wine, orange juice, orange zest, honey, stock, and cloves. Raise the heat to high and boil, stirring occasionally, until the sauce is reduced by about half, approximately 10 minutes.

3. Add a bit of the sauce to the arrowroot and stir until dissolved. Lower the heat and add the arrowroot mixture to the sauce. Continue cooking, stirring, until the sauce is thickened and glossy. Season with salt and pepper to taste. Add the duck and softened figs and cook until heated through. Serve immediately with the cooked spaghetti.

# TURKEY TETRAZZINI

**PREP TIME:** 25 MINUTES
**COOKING TIME:** 45 MINUTES
**SERVES:** 4

1 cup grated Gruyère or Swiss cheese
1 recipe hot White Sauce (page 82)
2 tablespoons sweet butter
1 small onion, minced
¾ pound white mushrooms, sliced
2 tablespoons sherry (or more, to taste)
Salt and freshly ground white pepper
1½ pounds boneless, skinless turkey breast,
    cut into 1-inch cubes
1 pound dried spaghetti, cooked according to
    package directions

1. Preheat oven to 375 degrees.

2. Stir the grated cheese into the hot white sauce and set aside.

3. Heat the butter in a sauté pan over medium heat. Add the onion and sauté until golden, about 5 minutes. Add the mushrooms and cook until softened, 5 to 7 minutes. Add the sherry and raise the heat to high. Cook 1 or 2 minutes longer. Season with salt and pepper to taste. Remove from heat and add to the white sauce.

4. Place the turkey cubes in a heatproof casserole or serving dish and add the white sauce with mushrooms. Bake, covered, in the preheated oven for 30 minutes, or until cooked through. Serve immediately with the spaghetti.

## SPAGHETTI WITH TURKEY IN MOLE SAUCE

*The making of an authentic mole—a sauce of ground nuts and spices—is, in Mexican cookery, a days-long process of grinding, toasting, simmering. This version incorporates the flavors of a traditional mole sauce but cooks in a matter of minutes. Either a spice grinder or a mini food processor would be useful for grinding the relatively small quantity of nuts and spices required.*

**PREP TIME:** 20 MINUTES
**COOKING TIME:** 20 MINUTES
**SERVES:** 4

¼ cup hulled pumpkin seeds
2 tablespoons sesame seeds
2 tablespoons raw almonds (about 10)
⅛ teaspoon EACH coriander seeds and anise
    seeds
3 whole cloves
10 peppercorns
6 tomatillos
2 garlic cloves
¼ cup water
Knifepoint of ground cinnamon

1 tablespoon ground red chili powder
2 tablespoons peanut oil
1 small onion, minced
1¼ pounds ground turkey breast
Salt and freshly ground black pepper
1 pound dried spaghetti, cooked according to
    package directions

1. In a 4-inch sauté pan, toast the pumpkin seeds, sesame seeds, and almonds over medium heat until they begin to brown and pop, about 2 or 3 minutes. Remove from the heat and let cool.

2. Combine the toasted seeds, coriander, anise, cloves, and peppercorns in the container of a blender or mini food processor. Pulse until finely ground. Remove and set aside. In the same container, place the tomatillos, garlic, and water. Pulse until smooth. Add the ground nut mixture, cinnamon, and chili powder to the container. Pulse until combined into a thick smooth paste.

3. Heat the peanut oil in a 9-inch sauté pan over medium heat. Add the onion and sauté until softened and translucent, about 5 minutes. Add the turkey, breaking it up with a spatula or wooden

spoon. Season with salt and pepper to taste and cook until the turkey is no longer pink, about 10 minutes. Add the spice paste to the turkey and mix until combined and heated through. Serve immediately with the cooked spaghetti.

## VARIATION

TURKEY IN CHOCOLATE MOLE SAUCE: Add 1½ tablespoons chocolate chips to the turkey at the end of Step 3. Stir until chocolate melts.

# MEAT SAUCES

From hearty, oven-braised stews to quick-cooked sautés, these sauces present a wide range of techniques and a variety of flavor combinations using beef, pork, lamb, and veal. You'll find that perennial favorite, spaghetti with meatballs, in this chapter (and a couple of variations on the meatball theme) along with savory Mexican- and spicy Middle Eastern-flavored dishes. Many of these are surprisingly versatile and make perfect party dishes—they can be doubled, made ahead of time, and frozen/reheated for a later date.

## SPAGHETTI WITH RICOTTA, HAM, AND BROCCOLI

**PREP TIME:** 10 MINUTES
**COOKING TIME:** 10 MINUTES
**SERVES:** 4

3 cups broccoli florets
Salt
2 tablespoons sweet butter
1 medium onion, minced
½ pound ham, diced
1 egg, lightly beaten
1 cup ricotta cheese
White pepper and nutmeg
1 pound dried spaghetti, cooked according to
    package directions

1. Cook the broccoli florets in salted boiling water until crisp-tender. Refresh in cold water and set aside.

2. Melt the butter in a 9-inch sauté pan over medium heat. Add the onion and sauté until golden and translucent, about 5 minutes. Add the ham and cook until heated through.

3. In a serving dish large enough to hold the pasta, combine the egg and ricotta cheese. Add the onion, ham, and broccoli florets and season with salt, white pepper, and ground nutmeg to taste.

4. Drain the cooked spaghetti and toss it with the ham and cheese mixture until thoroughly combined. Serve immediately.

# SPAGHETTI WITH BEEF BIRDS

*Beef birds or bracciole are a real home-style Italian-American dish. They do require a bit of preparation but are a delicious and soul-satisfying treat for a casual supper on a chilly autumn or winter day. If your supermarket doesn't sell beef cut in large thin slices, your butcher can certainly prepare the meat for you.*

**PREP TIME:** 30 MINUTES
**COOKING TIME:** 1 HOUR 10 MINUTES
**SERVES:** 4

2 ounces bacon, cut into lardons
1 large onion, minced
8 slices white bread, crusts removed and
    bread torn into small pieces
Fresh thyme
Salt and freshly ground black pepper
1 (13-ounce) can low-salt beef broth
1½ pounds top round (London broil), cut into
    4 thin slices
2 tablespoons safflower or canola oil
1 cup chopped fresh or canned tomatoes
½ cup dry red wine
2 tablespoons drained capers

1 bay leaf
1 tablespoon tomato paste
1 pound dried spaghetti, cooked according to
    package directions

1. Place the bacon in a 3½-quart ovenproof casserole over medium heat and cook until the bacon begins to render its fat. Add the onion and sauté until soft and translucent, about 5 minutes. Remove the bacon-onion mixture with a slotted spoon and set aside.

2. To make the stuffing for the bracciole, add ¾ cup of the onion mixture to the bread, along with 1 teaspoon fresh thyme and salt and pepper to taste. Add a little water or beef broth, a tablespoon at a time, until the stuffing just holds its shape when pressed together.

3. Preheat the oven to 350 degrees.

4. To prepare the beef birds: Place a slice of beef on the work surface and sprinkle it with black pepper. Place about ⅓ cup of stuffing in the center and fold over the ends (like a letter) to enclose it completely. Secure the sides with toothpicks. Repeat with the remaining beef and stuffing.

5.  Heat the oil in the ovenproof casserole over medium-high heat. Add the beef birds, in batches if necessary to avoid crowding, and brown them on all sides. Add the tomatoes, red wine, capers, bay leaf, and tomato paste, along with 3 sprigs of fresh thyme and the remaining onion-bacon mixture. Add enough beef broth just to cover the beef birds. Bring to a simmer. Remove the casserole from the heat. Cover and bake in the oven for 1 hour, or until the beef is cooked through.

6.  Serve with the cooked spaghetti.

# SPAGHETTI AND BEEF STEW

*Beef stew is such a well-loved and versatile dish that it adapts well to a wide variety of presentations, both plain and fancy—served over noodles or potatoes; baked in a crust; or as a French navarin. However, it's equally delicious and satisfying as a topping for spaghetti. If you wish, you can add cubed potatoes to the stew (or any other vegetables you like, such as green beans or peas) along with the carrots and turnips.*

**PREP TIME:** 20 MINUTES
**COOKING TIME:** 1½ HOURS
**SERVES:** 4

3 ounces bacon, cut into ¼ x 1-inch strips
1½ pounds stewing beef, cut into 1-inch cubes
¼ cup flour, seasoned with salt and pepper (for dredging the beef)
1 large onion, chopped
1 large celery stalk, chopped (½ cup)
1 tablespoon vegetable oil (if necessary)
1 cup dry red wine
½ a (28-ounce) can Italian plum tomatoes, with their juice
2 garlic cloves, minced
1 heaping tablespoon tomato paste
1 bay leaf
¼ teaspoon dried thyme
3 carrots, thinly sliced (about 2 cups)
1 small turnip, peeled and cut up (about 1 cup)
Salt and freshly ground black pepper
1 pound dried spaghetti, cooked according to package directions

1. Preheat the oven to 350 degrees.

2. Sauté the bacon in a 3½-quart casserole over medium heat until the fat begins to render. Remove the bacon with a slotted spoon and set aside.

3. Dredge the beef cubes in the seasoned flour. Shake off the excess flour and sauté the meat, in batches if necessary to prevent crowding, in the hot bacon fat until nicely browned. Remove with a slotted spoon and set aside.

4. Add the onion and celery to the pan, along with the tablespoon of oil if necessary to prevent sticking. Sauté the vegetables until soft and translucent, scraping up any browned bits on the bottom of the pan, about 5 to 7 minutes.

5. Add the remaining ingredients (except the salt and pepper and spaghetti), the bacon, and the beef to the pot. Bring the stew to a boil. Remove from the heat. Cover the casserole and bake in the oven for approximately 1 hour, or until the meat is tender. Season with salt and black pepper to taste. Serve with cooked spaghetti.

## VARIATION

SPAGHETTI AND LAMB STEW: Omit the bacon and substitute stewing lamb for the beef. Brown the lamb in 3 tablespoons vegetable oil. Add 1 sprig fresh rosemary to the stew as well. (Remove the rosemary sprig before serving.)

# SPAGHETTI WITH SMOKY CHILI

*One of my favorites is chili and spaghetti topped with grated Cheddar or Jack cheese. Sour cream, sliced pickled jalapeño peppers, and chopped red onion would also be delicious garnishes. Turn up the heat by adding additional hot peppers. (But remember, the longer the chili cooks, the more the heat in the chiles and cayenne pepper blooms.) This freezes well, too, so you might want to make a double batch.*

**PREP TIME:** 25 MINUTES
**COOKING TIME:** 2¼ HOURS
**SERVES:** 6 TO 8

6 slices bacon cut into ¼ x 1-inch strips
1 pound boneless pork, cut into 1-inch cubes
1½ pounds beef chuck, cut into 1-inch cubes
1 large red onion, minced
2 small green bell peppers, seeded and cubed
3 Anaheim chiles, seeded and sliced
2 jalapeño peppers, seeded and sliced
2 celery stalks, minced
4 minced garlic cloves
1 ham hock
1 (28-ounce) can tomatoes in purée
28 ounces water
1 tablespoon chili powder
1 bay leaf
1 teaspoon cumin
1 teaspoon dried oregano
½ teaspoon cayenne pepper (or more, to taste)
1 tablespoon rum
2 tablespoons fine cornmeal (masarepa or masa harina)
Salt and freshly ground black pepper
1½ pounds dried spaghetti, cooked according to package directions

1. Cook the bacon pieces in a 3½-quart casserole or Dutch oven over medium heat until the fat is rendered and the bacon translucent. Remove the bacon with a slotted spoon and set aside.

2. Add the pork and beef cubes to the bacon fat, in batches if necessary to prevent crowding, and cook over medium-high heat until nicely browned all over. Remove the meat with a slotted spoon and set aside.

3. Add the onion, fresh peppers, and celery to the pan and sauté over medium heat until softened, about 10 minutes. Return the bacon, pork, and beef to the pot and add the remaining ingredients except

for the cornmeal, salt and pepper, and spaghetti to the pan. Bring to a boil. Reduce the heat and simmer the stew, uncovered, for approximately 1½ to 2 hours, or until the meat is tender. Add the cornmeal and salt and pepper to taste. Simmer an additional 15 minutes, or until the sauce is slightly thickened.

4. Serve the chili over the spaghetti with any or all garnishes of your choice. (The garnishes can be served as side dishes.)

# SPAGHETTI WITH MEATBALLS

*Perhaps no other spaghetti dish figures so prominently in the American culinary psyche as spaghetti with meatballs. Our first dining-out experiences as toddlers—related by our parents with relish, in embarrassing detail, to prospective mates and in-laws at family get-togethers—inevitably involved flinging spaghetti and meatballs around some 1950s-style Italian joint replete with wax-dripped candles in wicker-covered wine bottles. We sang songs about it as kids: "On top of spaghetti/all covered with cheese/I lost my poor meatball . . ." (and you know how the rest of it goes).*

*Here are three recipes for that perennial favorite: one, a more traditional pork-beef version; another lighter, more contemporary version using ground turkey and veal; and the third an exotic sweet and spicy rendition based on African cuisine.*

*The following recipes make enough for at least 8 people and the meatballs freeze well for later use.*

**PREP TIME:** 10 MINUTES
**COOKING TIME:** 2 HOURS
**SERVES:** 8

# CLASSIC-STYLE MEATBALLS

4 slices firm-textured white bread, crusts
   removed
⅓ cup milk
1 pound ground beef
1 pound ground pork
1 egg, lightly beaten
1 teaspoon minced garlic
1 tablespoon minced fresh parsley
Salt and freshly ground black pepper
Olive or safflower oil for sautéing the
   meatballs
1 recipe Classic Italian Tomato Sauce (page 3)
1½ pounds dried spaghetti, cooked according
   to package directions
Freshly grated Parmesan or Romano cheese

1. In a medium-sized mixing bowl, combine the bread and milk. Mash lightly with a fork until all the milk is absorbed and the bread is broken up.

2. Add the beef, pork, egg, garlic, parsley, and salt and pepper and toss lightly with a fork until thoroughly combined. Taste the meatball mixture for seasoning by frying a spoonful in a small saute

pan until cooked through and no longer pink. Adjust for seasoning.

3. Heat $\frac{1}{4}$ inch of oil in a large sauté pan over medium-high heat. Shape the meat mixture into meatballs using a $\frac{1}{4}$-cup measure. Place the meatballs into the hot oil and sauté them until nicely browned on all sides. (Shaking the pan as the meatballs cook helps to prevent them from sticking.)

4. Gently heat the tomato sauce in a large saucepan. Remove the meatballs with a slotted spoon and place them in the pot of tomato sauce. Simmer, uncovered, over very low heat for 2 hours.

5. Serve over spaghetti, sprinkled with the grated cheese.

# SAGE-FLAVORED TURKEY AND VEAL MEATBALLS

**PREP TIME:** 10 MINUTES
**COOKING TIME:** 2 HOURS
**SERVES:** 8

1 pound ground veal
1¼ pounds ground turkey
1 egg, lightly beaten
1 teaspoon ground sage (more or less, to
  taste)
1 teaspoon salt
1 teaspoon minced garlic
⅓ cup wheat germ
¼ cup coarsely grated Pecorino Romano
  cheese
Olive oil for sautéing the meatballs
1½ pounds dried spaghetti, cooked according
  to package directions
1 recipe Classic Italian Tomato Sauce (page 3)
Freshly grated Parmesan or Romano cheese

1. Combine the veal, turkey, egg, sage, salt, garlic, wheat germ, and ¼ cup cheese in a large bowl. Mix thoroughly. Taste the meatball mixture for seasoning by frying a spoonful in a small sauté pan until cooked through and no longer pink. Taste and adjust for seasoning.

2. Heat ¼ inch of olive oil in a large sauté pan over medium-high heat. Shape the meat mixture into meatballs using a ¼-cup measure. Place the meatballs in the hot oil and sauté them until nicely browned on all sides. (Shaking the pan as the meatballs cook helps to prevent them from sticking.)

3. Gently heat the tomato sauce in a large saucepan. Remove the meatballs with a slotted spoon and place them in the pot of tomato sauce. Simmer, uncovered, over very low heat for 2 hours.

4. Serve the sauce over the cooked spaghetti and sprinkle with the grated cheese.

# AFRICAN LAMB MEATBALLS

**PREP TIME:** 25 MINUTES
**COOKING TIME:** 1 HOUR
**SERVES:** 4

## FOR THE MEATBALLS

1¼ **pounds lean ground lamb**
1 **small onion, minced**
1 **garlic clove, minced**
1 **egg**
½ **cup dry breadcrumbs**
⅓ **cup chopped dried apricots**
**Salt and pepper to taste**
¼ **cup safflower oil**

## FOR THE SAUCE

1 **small onion, minced**
1 **medium tart green apple (such as Granny**
   **Smith), peeled and thinly sliced**
1 **(13¾-ounce) can beef broth**
1 **small banana, sliced**
1½ **tablespoons curry powder**
⅛ **teaspoon cinnamon**
1 **tablespoon tomato paste**

1 **pound spaghetti, cooked according to**
   **package directions**
**Yogurt (optional garnish)**
**Chopped fresh mint leaves (optional garnish)**

1. For the meatballs: Combine all the ingredients except the oil in a bowl. Toss thoroughly and taste for seasoning by frying a small amount of the meat mixture in a sauté pan. Shape the meat into 20 to 24 two-inch meatballs.

2. Heat the oil in a 3½-quart Dutch oven over medium heat. Add the meatballs, in batches if necessary to prevent crowding, and brown on all sides. Remove the meatballs with a slotted spoon and set aside.

3. Make the sauce: Add the onion and apple to the pan, scraping up any browned bits from the bottom, and sauté until golden and translucent, about 5 or 6 minutes. Add the meatballs, beef broth, banana, curry powder, cinnamon, and tomato paste to the pan. Simmer, partially covered, for approximately 45 minutes, or until the meatballs are cooked through.

4. Serve over cooked spaghetti. Garnish with yogurt and chopped fresh mint leaves, if desired.

## SPAGHETTI WITH PORK IN GREEN SAUCE

*This recipe uses the green tomatoes called tomatillos. They are not members of the tomato family at all, but belong to the gooseberry family. Look for those that are firm, green, and blemish-free.*

**PREP TIME:** 10 MINUTES
**COOKING TIME:** 1¼ HOURS
**SERVES:** 4

½ **pound tomatillos, husked**
1½ **tablespoons lime juice**
1 **garlic clove**
1 **small onion, cut up**
2 **fresh jalapeño peppers, stemmed and seeded**
6 **sprigs fresh cilantro**
4 **sprigs fresh flat-leaf parsley**
1 **teaspoon sugar**
½ **teaspoon salt**
2 **tablespoons peanut oil**
1½ **pounds boneless pork butt, cut into 1-inch cubes**
½ **cup water**
2 **small zucchini, cut into ½-inch-thick slices**

1 **pound dried spaghetti, cooked according to package directions**

1. Purée the first 9 ingredients in the container of a food processor or blender until smooth.

2. Heat the oil in a 3½-quart casserole over medium-high heat. Sauté the pork cubes, in batches if necessary to prevent crowding, until nicely browned on all sides. Add the tomatillo sauce and water to the pork. Bring the mixture to a boil. Reduce the heat to a simmer and cook, uncovered, for an hour, stirring occasionally.

3. Add the zucchini to the pan. Cover and steam until the zucchini is crisp-tender, about 5 minutes. If the sauce is too thin, remove the cover and cook a bit longer to let some of the extra liquid evaporate.

4. Serve the sauce over the cooked spaghetti

# SPAGHETTI WITH PORK AND HOT PEPPERS

*There's a saying that some like it hot. You know them. That group out there who, if they had their druthers, would drench everything in one of the dozens of different hot pepper sauces they purchase as collectibles. They are the type who, when presented with a carefully balanced, lovingly seasoned culinary delicacy, inevitably request the bottle of Tabasco—and seem genuinely surprised when the deflated cook refuses it. Well, here's the dish for the hot pepper set. You can crank up the heat to tongue-numbing proportions by adjusting the amount of chili oil used. If you cannot find the tiny Italian red peperoncini packed in oil, you can substitute another type of chili oil or chili paste.*

**PREP TIME:** 5 MINUTES
**COOKING TIME:** 30 MINUTES
**SERVES:** 4

1¼ pounds center-cut pork chops
   (approximately 4 half-inch-thick chops)
2 tablespoons olive oil
1 small jar hot red peperoncini packed in oil
1 small jar pickled green jalapeño peppers
   packed in vinegar
¾ cup chicken stock
1 pound dried spaghetti, cooked according to
   package directions

1. Remove the bones from the pork chops and cut the meat into 1-inch cubes. Reserve the bones.

2. Heat the olive oil and 2 teaspoons of oil from the hot peppers in a large (3½-quart) casserole over medium-high heat. Add the pork cubes and bones, in batches if necessary to prevent crowding, and sauté until browned on all sides. Lower the heat and add ⅓ cup juice from the jalapeño peppers and the chicken stock to the pork.

3. Simmer, covered, over low heat until cooked through, approximately 20 to 25 minutes. Remove the bones, toss with the hot cooked spaghetti, and garnish with the red and green hot peppers.

## SPAGHETTI WITH MOROCCAN LAMB SAUSAGE AND VEGETABLES

**PREP TIME:** 15 MINUTES
**COOKING TIME:** 25 MINUTES
**SERVES:** 4

Salt
1 medium zucchini, cut into ¼-inch dice
1 medium yellow (summer) squash, cut into
    ¼-inch dice
1 tablespoon safflower or canola oil
1 pound Merguez (spicy lamb) sausage, cut
    into 2-inch pieces
1 cup beef broth
1½ teaspoons curry powder
¾ teaspoon ground cumin
½ teaspoon hot red pepper flakes, or to taste
1 (16-ounce) can chick-peas, drained
Freshly ground black pepper
1 pound dried spaghetti, cooked according to
    package directions

1. In a 2-quart saucepan, bring to a boil enough salted water to cover the zucchini and yellow squash. Cook the squashes until crisp-tender, approximately 1 to 2 minutes. Drain and refresh with cold water.

2. Heat the oil in a 9-inch sauté pan over medium heat. Add the sausage and cook until browned on all sides. Add the beef broth, curry, cumin, and hot pepper to the sausage. Taste and adjust for seasoning. Lower the heat and simmer, partially covered, until the sausage is cooked through, approximately 20 minutes.

3. Add the yellow and green squashes and the chick-peas to the sausage and cook until heated through. Season with salt and pepper to taste. Serve immediately over the cooked spaghetti.

# SPAGHETTI WITH ITALIAN SAUSAGE AND PEPPERS

**PREP TIME:** 15 MINUTES
**COOKING TIME:** 40 MINUTES
**SERVES:** 4 TO 6

8 sweet or hot Italian sausages (about 1½
    pounds), cut into ½-inch slices
2 tablespoons vegetable oil
1 large onion, thinly sliced
1 large green bell pepper, seeded and thinly
    sliced
1 large red bell pepper, seeded and thinly
    sliced
1 yellow bell pepper, seeded and thinly sliced
1½ teaspoons minced garlic
½ teaspoon black pepper
1 teaspoon salt
1½ teaspoons balsamic vinegar
1 pound dried spaghetti, cooked according to
    package directions

1. Sauté the sausage slices in a 9-inch sauté pan over medium heat until cooked through and no longer pink, about 8 to 10 minutes. Remove the sausage slices with a slotted spoon. Set aside and keep warm.

2. Add the oil to the pan in which the sausages were cooked. Add the onion and bell peppers and cook until softened, approximately 10 minutes. Add the garlic, black pepper, salt, and vinegar and cook, uncovered, over medium heat, stirring occasionally, until the peppers and onions are very soft and lightly browned, approximately 20 minutes.

3. Add the sausages to the pepper mixture. Taste and adjust for seasoning. Serve immediately over the cooked spaghetti.

## VARIATION

VEAL AND PEPPERS: Substitute 1 pound veal cutlets, thinly sliced, for the sausages. Skip Step 1 above and proceed with Step 2. After the bell peppers and onions have cooked, remove them from the pan with a slotted spoon. Sauté the veal slices briefly, about 3 to 5 minutes, until cooked through. Combine with the pepper-onion mixture and serve over the spaghetti.

# SPAGHETTI WITH VEAL IN PORT WINE SAUCE

**PREP TIME:** 10 MINUTES
**COOKING TIME:** 10 MINUTES
**SERVES:** 4

1 tablespoon olive oil
1 tablespoon safflower oil
¾ pound veal scaloppine, cut into strips
1 small onion, minced
1 garlic clove, minced
1 tablespoon flour
¾ cup veal or chicken stock
2 tablespoons port wine
1 teaspoon freshly squeezed lemon juice
Salt and freshly ground black pepper
8 canned or bottled artichoke hearts,
    quartered
1 pound dried spaghetti, cooked according to
    package directions

1. Heat the olive and safflower oil in a 9-inch skillet over medium-high heat. Add the veal strips and sauté until browned, approximately 1 to 2 minutes. Do not overcook! Remove the veal from the skillet with a slotted spoon and set aside, covered.

2. Add the onion and garlic to the sauté pan. Sauté 1 to 2 minutes, stirring to scrape up any browned bits. Add the flour, stirring constantly for 2 or 3 minutes. Lower the heat and add the stock, port, and lemon juice. Season with salt and pepper to taste. Add the artichoke hearts and veal strips to the sauce and cook until just heated through. Serve immediately over the cooked spaghetti.

# SPAGHETTI WITH VEAL AND SPINACH

**PREP TIME:** 15 MINUTES
**COOKING TIME:** 15 MINUTES
**SERVES:** 4

1 pound spinach, stemmed and rinsed
2 tablespoons safflower or canola oil
1 medium onion, minced
1 large garlic clove, minced
1¼ pounds ground veal
2 tablespoons dry vermouth
1 cup heavy cream
Freshly grated nutmeg
Salt and white pepper
1 pound dried spaghetti, cooked according to
    package directions
Grated Parmesan and Romano cheese

1.  Place the spinach with the water clinging to its leaves in a 9-inch sauté pan. Cover and cook until wilted, about 2 or 3 minutes. Drain and refresh with cold water. When cool enough to handle, squeeze all excess water from the spinach and chop fine. Set aside.

2.  Heat the oil in a 9-inch sauté pan over medium heat. Add the onion and garlic and cook until golden and translucent, about 5 minutes. Add the veal and sauté until cooked through and no longer pink.

3.  Turn the heat to high and add the vermouth and cream. Cook 2 minutes. Lower the heat and add 1 cup of chopped spinach. Season with nutmeg, salt, and white pepper to taste. Serve over spaghetti with the grated cheeses.

# FROM THE SEA

This chapter highlights fresh fish and shellfish—from a delicate scalloped salmon almondine to a spicy, peppery red clam sauce. (You might also wish to check the index and chapter 6 for other seafood ideas.)

One thing that's important with fish cookery is to overcome fear of fire. A relatively high flame cooks seafood more quickly, but also ensures that the fish or shellfish remains tender, because after more than a few minutes on the stove, shellfish in particular will toughen up and become less palatable.

Another key to successful fish cookery is proper cleaning. Always wash mussels and clams thoroughly in several changes of water to remove grit and extraneous matter, and check your fish for stray bones and scales.

# SPAGHETTI WITH "CONFETTI" OYSTERS

**PREP TIME:** 10 MINUTES
**COOKING TIME:** 20 MINUTES
**SERVES:** 4

3 tablespoons sweet butter
1 small onion, minced
1 celery stalk, minced
1 small red bell pepper, seeded and diced
  (about ¾ cup)
1½ cups corn kernels, preferably fresh
1 teaspoon dried thyme
1½ cups heavy cream
Freshly ground white pepper
12 ounces fresh shucked oysters OR 1
  (12-ounce) can oysters, drained
Salt
1 pound dried spaghetti, cooked according to
  package directions

1. Melt the butter in a 9-inch sauté pan over medium heat. Add the onion, celery, red bell pepper, corn kernels, and thyme and sauté until softened, about 8 to 10 minutes.

2. Add the cream and white pepper to taste. Turn the heat to high and boil until the cream is reduced and thick enough to coat the back of a spoon, about 10 minutes. Lower the heat. Add the oysters and simmer until cooked through, about 3 to 5 minutes. Season with salt to taste. Serve immediately over the cooked spaghetti.

# SPAGHETTI WITH WHITE CLAM SAUCE

**PREP TIME:** 20 MINUTES
**COOKING TIME:** 10 MINUTES
**SERVES:** 4

2 dozen littleneck clams
½ cup minced shallot (1 to 2 large)
1 garlic clove, minced
2 tablespoons chopped flat-leaf parsley
1 tablespoon freshly squeezed lemon juice
½ cup dry white wine
1 cup water
1 teaspoon salt
2 tablespoons sweet butter
1 pound dried spaghetti, cooked according to
    package directions

1. Scrub the clams to remove all sand and dirt. Wash in at least 3 changes of clean cold water and set aside. (If you need to keep the clams for more than a few minutes, place them in the refrigerator in a bowl of cold water with a bit of flour or cornmeal sprinkled on the surface. Rinse thoroughly before using.)

2. Place the shallots, garlic, parsley, lemon juice, white wine, water, salt, and butter in a 4-quart saucepan over medium-high heat. Bring to a boil and simmer for 5 minutes. (This much of the recipe can be prepared ahead of time.) Lower the heat. Add the clams in a single layer to the liquid. Cover and simmer until the clams just begin to open, about 5 minutes.

3. When the clams are cool enough to handle, remove the clam meat from the shells, being very careful to catch all of the juices in a bowl. Coarsely chop the clams.

4. Return the clam meat and juice to the cooking liquid. Reheat if necessary. Toss with the cooked spaghetti.

## VARIATION

RED CLAM SAUCE: Prepare the sauce for Spaghetti all' Arrabbiata (page 2). Follow master recipe here through Step 3. Put the clam meat into the arrabbiata sauce with their juices. Reheat, if necessary, very gently. (You don't want to overcook and toughen the clam meat.) Toss with the cooked spaghetti.

# SPAGHETTI WITH SHRIMP "MARGARITA"

**PREP TIME:** 30 MINUTES
**COOKING TIME:** 10 MINUTES
**SERVES:** 4

¼ cup olive oil
1¼ pounds medium or large shrimp, peeled
    and deveined
2 teaspoons chopped garlic
2 tablespoons freshly squeezed lime juice
2 tablespoons tequila
1½ teaspoons Triple Sec liqueur
1 teaspoon salt
Freshly ground black pepper
Grated zest of 1 lime
1 pound dried spaghetti, cooked according to
    package directions

1. Heat the olive oil in a 9-inch sauté pan over medium-high heat. Add the shrimp and sauté until pink and cooked through, 3 to 4 minutes, depending upon the size of the shrimp.

2. Add the garlic, lime juice, tequila, and Triple Sec. Cook 2 or 3 minutes more, tossing the shrimp occasionally. Season with the salt and black pepper to taste. Add the lime zest to the shrimp. Serve immediately with the cooked spaghetti.

## SPAGHETTI WITH SHRIMP AND SCALLOPS

**PREP TIME:** 20 MINUTES
**COOKING TIME:** 10 MINUTES
**SERVES:** 4

2 tablespoons sweet butter
2 tablespoons safflower or canola oil
¾ pound medium shrimp, peeled and
    deveined
¾ pound bay or sea scallops, halved or
    quartered if large
3 or 4 garlic cloves, minced
1 small bunch flat-leaf parsley, minced
Salt and freshly ground black pepper
1 pound dried spaghetti, cooked according to
    package directions

1. Melt the butter and oil in a 9-inch sauté pan over medium-high heat. Add the shrimp and scallops and sauté, tossing occasionally, until cooked through, about 3 to 5 minutes.

2. Add the garlic, parsley, salt, and freshly ground black pepper to taste. Serve immediately over the cooked spaghetti.

## VARIATION

FISHERMAN'S SAUCE: Add to the sautéed shrimp and scallops ⅓ pound firm-fleshed white fish, cut into small pieces. Sauté an additional 1 to 2 minutes, or until the fish is cooked through.

# SPAGHETTI WITH FISH CAKES

*Friday was always fish cake and spaghetti day in the grade school cafeteria. There was no mistaking that special aroma of fried fish and sweet tomato sauce (to be served over glutinous spaghetti) that filled the air. Even today, I'm afraid, I can conjure up that olfactory memory. Well, these crunchy cod or salmon cakes are a far cry from our childhood memories. Serve the cod cakes with Spaghetti with Green Herb Butter (page 102) or Marinara Sauce (page 3). The salmon cakes would be terrific with the Spaghetti with Sauce Rémoulade on page 114.*

## SALMON CAKES

**PREP TIME:** 20 MINUTES
**COOKING TIME:** 10 MINUTES
**SERVES:** 4

1 white waxy potato (about ¼ pound), peeled
    and cut up
1 pound chilled salmon fillet, skinned and cut
    into chunks
1 egg white
1 shallot, minced
1 tablespoon minced chives
½ teaspoon salt
1 teaspoon freshly squeezed lemon juice
Corn oil, safflower oil, or canola oil for frying
Fresh breadcrumbs
1 pound dried spaghetti, cooked according to
    package directions
Sauce of your choice (see suggestions above)

1. Cook the potato in water until tender. Mash thoroughly and cool to room temperature.

2. Place the salmon chunks in the container of a food processor or blender and pulse until finely chopped. Add the potato, egg white, shallot, chives, salt, and lemon juice and combine thoroughly.

3. Heat ½ inch of oil in a 9-inch sauté pan over medium-high heat. While the oil is heating, form the salmon cakes, using a ⅛-cup measure. Roll them in breadcrumbs to coat evenly. Sauté the salmon cakes, a few at a time, in the hot oil until nicely browned, about 2 minutes per side. Drain on paper towels and keep warm until ready to serve with the cooked spaghetti and sauce of your choice.

# COD CAKES

**PREP TIME:** 30 MINUTES
**COOKING TIME:** 15 MINUTES
**SERVES:** 4

1 pound firm-fleshed white fish such as cod,
    scrod, or halibut, cut into chunks
¼ cup minced onion
1 tablespoon chopped fresh dill weed
1 egg
Salt and pepper
Corn oil or safflower oil for frying
Fresh breadcrumbs
1 pound dried spaghetti, cooked according to
    package directions
Sauce of your choice (see suggestions on
    page 61)

1. Place the fish chunks in the container of a blender or food processor and pulse until finely chopped. Add the onion, dill, egg, and salt and pepper to taste and pulse until all ingredients are thoroughly combined. Chill the fish mixture for 15 to 20 minutes.

2. Heat approximately ½ inch of oil in a 9-inch sauté pan over medium-high heat.

3. While the oil is heating, shape the fish into 8 cakes using a ¼-cup measure. Roll the fish cakes in the breadcrumbs until evenly coated. When the oil is hot, add the fish cakes and cook 2 to 3 minutes per side. Drain on paper towels and serve immediately with the spaghetti and sauce of your choice.

# SPAGHETTI WITH SCALLOPED SALMON

**PREP TIME:** 10 MINUTES
**COOKING TIME:** 15 MINUTES
**SERVES:** 4

1¼ pounds salmon fillet, skinned and cut into
    1-inch cubes
Salt and white pepper
1½ cups heavy cream
2 tablespoons fresh minced herbs, such as
    dill weed, tarragon, parsley, chervil, or
    other
Grated nutmeg
⅔ cup sliced blanched almonds
½ cup freshly grated Parmesan cheese
1 pound dried spaghetti, cooked according to
    package directions

1. Preheat the oven to 350 degrees.

2. Place the salmon in a baking dish and season lightly with salt and white pepper. Add the cream, fresh herbs, and nutmeg to the salmon. Toss to combine. Bake, covered, in the preheated oven for 10 minutes, or until the fish is cooked to the desired degree of doneness.

3. Top the fish with the almonds and Parmesan cheese. Run the baking dish under the broiler for a minute or two until the top is browned and bubbling.

4. Spoon the salmon and sauce over the cooked spaghetti and serve immediately.

## SPAGHETTI WITH FRESH SARDINE SAUCE

*If you're a real sardine fan, this is the sauce for you. The fresh sardines, while requiring extra preparation (unless you have a kind fishmonger who will clean them for you), yield a much more delicate flavor than the canned version, though they can be used in a pinch.*

**PREP TIME:** 30 MINUTES
**COOKING TIME:** 15 MINUTES
**SERVES:** 4

3 tablespoons olive oil
1 celery stalk, minced
½ green bell pepper, seeded and diced (about
    ¾ cup)
1 small onion, minced
1 teaspoon minced garlic
1 cup chopped tomatoes, preferably fresh
2 tablespoons minced flat-leaf parsley
1 pound fresh sardines, cleaned and boned,*
    or 2 (3¾-ounce) cans, drained
1 tablespoon freshly squeezed lemon juice
2 tablespoons balsamic vinegar
Salt and freshly ground black pepper

1 pound dried spaghetti, cooked according to
    package directions

1. Heat the oil in a 9-inch sauté pan over medium heat. Add the celery, green pepper, onion, garlic, tomatoes, and parsley and sauté until softened, about 8 to 10 minutes. Add the sardines, lemon juice, vinegar, and salt and black pepper to taste.

2. Sauté the sardines until cooked through, about 5 minutes. Serve immediately over the cooked spaghetti.

* To clean fresh sardines: Cut the head and tail off the sardine, slicing on the diagonal. Make a slice across the belly and remove the entrails. Grasp the spine of the fish at the head end and pull gently to remove. Slice the sardine into 4 pieces.

# SPAGHETTI WITH SEAFOOD AND CHUNKY GAZPACHO SAUCE

*This Spanish-style dish would be terrific with any type of firm-fleshed fish steak or shrimp. While the recipe calls for sautéing the fish, you could grill it as well. Brush the fish steaks or shrimp with the olive oil, season with salt and pepper, and grill as you normally would. To serve, cut the fish into bite-sized pieces and serve over spaghetti with the sauce. Using a food processor to chop the vegetables is easy and quick, but you want to make sure not to overdo it. The vegetables should be fairly chunky to lend texture to the dish. Note that the uncooked sauce is served at room temperature.*

**PREP TIME:** 20 MINUTES
**COOKING TIME:** 10 MINUTES
**SERVES:** 4

## FOR THE SAUCE

3 medium tomatoes, chopped (about 2 cups)
1 cucumber, seeded and chopped (about 1 cup)
2 tablespoons chopped onion
1 celery stalk, chopped (about ¼ cup)
½ green bell pepper, seeded and chopped (about ⅓ cup)
1 tablespoon EACH minced fresh parsley and basil
1 teaspoon minced fresh cilantro
1 garlic clove, chopped
Salt and pepper to taste

## FOR THE FISH

¼ cup olive oil
1½ pounds firm-fleshed fish steaks, such as swordfish, tuna, or mako, cut into bite-sized pieces, OR 1½ pounds rock shrimp or shrimp
Salt and pepper
1 pound dried spaghetti, cooked according to package directions

1. Combine all the sauce ingredients in a serving dish and set aside at room temperature.

2. Heat the oil in a sauté pan over medium-high heat. Add the seafood pieces and sauté until cooked through, about 3 to 4 minutes. Serve over the cooked spaghetti with the gazpacho sauce.

## SPAGHETTI WITH MEDITERRANEAN TUNA SAUCE

**PREP TIME:** 15 MINUTES
**COOKING TIME:** 15 MINUTES
**SERVES:** 4

3 tablespoons olive oil
1 small onion, minced
1 celery stalk, minced
1 pound fresh tuna, cut into small
    (½- to ¾-inch) cubes
1½ teaspoons minced garlic
1 tablespoon minced flat-leaf parsley
½ tablespoon tomato paste
⅓ cup pitted black olives (preferably niçoise
    or Greek, not California)
3 anchovy fillets, cut up
1 tablespoon capers
2 tablespoons shredded fresh basil
Salt and freshly ground black pepper
1 pound dried spaghetti, cooked according to
    package directions

1.  Heat the olive oil in a 9-inch sauté pan over medium heat. Add the onion and celery and sauté until softened and translucent, about 8 to 10 minutes. Add the tuna, garlic, and parsley to the pan. Sauté until the tuna is cooked through, approximately 5 to 6 minutes (shorter or longer, depending on how rare you like your tuna).

2.  Add the tomato paste, olives, anchovies, capers, and basil to the tuna and heat through. Season with salt and pepper to taste. Serve immediately over the cooked spaghetti.

# ORIENT EXPRESS

We've become so accustomed to associating oriental food with rice that pairing these dishes with spaghetti may seem a bit odd at first. But a wide variety of noodles, whether made from soy, rice, or wheat flours, appear in Asian cookery, particularly in China where, even today, noodle making is a venerable art form.

In this chapter you'll find recipes borrowing from the cuisines of Asia—China, Thailand, Japan, India, and even the Philippines. Because of our growing familiarity with Asian cookery and its increasing popularity, just about all of the ingredients used, even exotica like unsweetened coconut milk, mango chutney, and black bean sauce, are readily available in supermarkets and ethnic grocery stores nationwide. Another added, and perhaps more important, feature: in a wok or wok sauté pan, these recipes cook in minutes, literally in the time it takes to drop your spaghetti in boiling water and cook it.

## SPAGHETTI WITH CHICKEN CHOW MEIN

**PREP TIME:** 15 MINUTES
**COOKING TIME:** 10 MINUTES
**SERVES:** 4

1 tablespoon cornstarch
1 tablespoon dry sherry or rice wine
¼ cup water
1 egg white, lightly beaten
2 large chicken breasts, skinned, boned, and
   thinly sliced
3 tablespoons peanut oil
2 garlic cloves, minced
1 one-inch piece fresh ginger, peeled and
   minced
1 medium onion, sliced
3 celery stalks, thinly sliced on the diagonal
½ pound fresh button mushrooms, stemmed
3 tablespoons soy sauce
½ cup fresh mung bean sprouts
1 pound dried spaghetti, cooked according to
   package directions

1. Dissolve the cornstarch in the sherry and water. Mix until smooth and set aside. Toss together the egg white and chicken slices and set aside while preparing the other ingredients.

2. Heat the peanut oil in a wok or high-sided sauté pan over high heat. Add the garlic, ginger, and onion and stir-fry until aromatic, 1 or 2 minutes. Add the celery and stir-fry 1 or 2 minutes; add the mushrooms and stir-fry until softened and almost cooked through. Add the chicken slices to the wok and stir-fry until the chicken is cooked through. Stir the cornstarch mixture, add it and the soy sauce, and cook until sauce is thick and glossy. Add the bean sprouts and toss to combine. Serve immediately with the cooked spaghetti.

# SPAGHETTI AND CHICKEN WITH HOT CHILES AND BASIL

*This spicy Thai-style dish would be terrific with sliced beef or pork, too. The fish sauce called for in the recipe and the recipe for Shrimp with Vegetables in Coconut Milk with Spaghetti on page 77 is the Thai all-purpose seasoning prepared from fermented anchovies. While it does smell a bit funky in the bottle, it really adds a special flavor to the food. Use it liberally. Lemongrass is increasingly available in the produce section of supermarkets. If you don't find it there, you can get it in an oriental market.*

**PREP TIME:** 10 MINUTES
**COOKING TIME:** 10 MINUTES
**SERVES:** 4

¼ cup peanut oil
1 bunch (4 large or 6 small) scallions, thinly sliced (white and 2 inches of green)
1 one-inch piece fresh ginger, peeled and minced
1 stalk lemongrass, thinly sliced
2 garlic cloves, minced
4 jalapeño peppers, seeded and thinly sliced
1 pound boneless, skinless chicken breasts, thinly sliced
Juice from 1 lime (about 3 tablespoons)
Thai fish sauce (nam pla)
½ cup fresh whole basil leaves (16 to 20 large)
1 pound dried spaghetti, cooked according to package directions

1. Heat the oil in a wok over medium-high heat. Add the scallions, ginger, lemongrass, and garlic and stir-fry until aromatic, about 1 or 2 minutes. Add the jalapeño peppers and cook until softened, about 1 or 2 minutes.

2. Add the chicken slices and lime juice and stir-fry until the chicken is cooked through and no longer pink, about 3 to 5 minutes. Add fish sauce to taste.

3. Stir in the basil leaves and cook until just wilted. Serve immediately over the cooked spaghetti.

# SPAGHETTI WITH COCONUT SHRIMP IN DUCK SAUCE

*This dish is really delicious. When you add the shrimp to the wok, make sure they are at room temperature and the wok is good and hot. Also, stir-fry enthusiastically, because you need to cook the shrimp rapidly and without sticking to prevent the coconut from burning.*

**PREP TIME:** 30 MINUTES
**COOKING TIME:** 10 MINUTES
**SERVES:** 4

FOR THE SHRIMP

**2 egg whites**
**2 tablespoons water**
**¼ cup cornstarch**
**½ teaspoon salt**
**⅓ cup grated unsweetened coconut**
**¾ pound medium shrimp (about 3 dozen), peeled and deveined**

FOR THE SAUCE

**¼ cup peanut oil**
**1 one-inch piece fresh ginger, peeled and minced**
**6 scallions, thinly sliced**
**2 garlic cloves, minced**
**1 large red bell pepper, seeded and diced**
**6 tablespoons prepared Chinese duck sauce**
**1 pound dried spaghetti, cooked according to package directions**

1. In a shallow dish, beat the egg whites and water. Gradually whisk in the cornstarch, salt, and coconut until well combined (you may need to add a bit more water if the mixture is too thick). Mix in the shrimp and toss until thoroughly coated. Set aside while preparing the sauce.

2. Heat the oil in a wok over high heat. Add the ginger, scallions, and garlic and stir-fry until aromatic, 1 or 2 minutes. Add the red pepper and stir-fry another 2 to 3 minutes, until softened.

3. Add the shrimp and stir-fry another 2 or 3 minutes, until the shrimp are cooked through. Add the duck sauce and toss to combine. Serve immediately over the cooked spaghetti.

# SPAGHETTI WITH MANGO CHICKEN

**PREP TIME:** 10 MINUTES
**COOKING TIME:** 15 MINUTES
**SERVES:** 4

1 one-inch piece ginger, peeled and minced
1 garlic clove, minced
1 cup plain yogurt
2 tablespoons curry powder
2 tablespoons peanut oil
1 large onion, cut into chunks
2 large celery stalks, thinly sliced on the
    diagonal
2 jalapeño peppers, seeded and thinly sliced
    (optional)
4 boneless, skinless chicken breasts, thinly
    sliced
½ cup mango chutney
1 pound dried spaghetti, cooked according to
    package directions

1. Combine the ginger, garlic, yogurt, and curry powder in a small bowl.

2. Heat the oil in a wok or high-sided skillet over medium-high heat. Add the onion, celery, and jalapeño peppers, if desired, and cook until softened, about 5 minutes. Add the chicken slices and stir-fry until the pieces are firm on the outside but not quite cooked through, about 2 to 3 minutes.

3. Lower the heat and add the yogurt mixture and chutney to the chicken and vegetables. Simmer until cooked through, about 5 minutes. Serve immediately over the cooked spaghetti.

## SPAGHETTI WITH MUSSELS IN BLACK BEAN SAUCE

*This is a version of a fabulous dish I used to get in New York's Chinatown at a restaurant remarkable only for its utter lack of decor and unbelievably surly service. I can't emphasize how important it is to wash, wash, wash shellfish in at least 3 changes of clean cold water to remove mud, sand, and whatever else is clinging to the shells There's nothing worse than sitting down to a beautiful plate of shellfish and tasting a mouthful of grit. This recipe would also work wonderfully with clams.*

**PREP TIME:** 20 MINUTES
**COOKING TIME:** 10 MINUTES
**SERVES:** 4 TO 6

3 tablespoons peanut oil
2 garlic cloves, minced
6 scallions (white and 1 inch of green), thinly
    sliced
1 one-inch piece fresh ginger, peeled and
    minced
2 large jalapeño peppers, peeled and thinly
    sliced
2 tablespoons rice wine

¼ cup soy sauce
4 dozen mussels, debearded and scrubbed
¼ cup prepared black bean sauce
1 pound dried spaghetti, cooked according to
    package directions

1. Heat the oil in a wok over medium-high heat. Add the garlic, scallions, ginger, and jalapeño peppers and cook until aromatic, about 1 to 2 minutes. Add the rice wine and soy sauce and stir to blend.

2. Place the mussels in the wok. Lower heat slightly and cook the mussels, covered, until they begin to open, about 5 to 7 minutes. (Discard any mussels that do not open.) Add the black bean sauce and toss with the mussels. Serve with the cooked spaghetti.

# PICKLED BEEF AND CABBAGE WITH SPAGHETTI

**PREP TIME:** 15 MINUTES
**COOKING TIME:** 15 MINUTES
**SERVES:** 4

⅔ cup soy sauce
¼ cup white vinegar
2 garlic cloves, minced
1 tablespoon tamarind paste (available in Asian and oriental markets)
½ teaspoon black pepper
1 pound beef, cut into ½-inch cubes
¼ cup peanut oil
1 large onion, thinly sliced
1 pound Chinese cabbage (bok choy), thinly sliced
1 pound dried spaghetti, cooked according to package directions

1. Combine the soy sauce, vinegar, garlic, tamarind paste, and black pepper with the beef cubes in a nonreactive bowl or container. Marinate overnight in the refrigerator.

2. Bring the meat to room temperature before cooking. Drain and pat the meat dry. Reserve the marinade.

3. Heat the peanut oil in a wok or deep sauté pan over high heat. Add the meat cubes to the hot oil and stir-fry until cooked through and nicely browned, approximately 5 to 7 minutes. Remove the meat with a slotted spoon and set it aside.

4. Add the onion to the pan and stir-fry until soft and wilted. Add the cabbage and the reserved marinade and cook until the cabbage is wilted and the liquid is slightly reduced. Add the beef and toss with the vegetables until combined and heated through. Serve immediately over the cooked spaghetti.

## PORK, MUSHROOMS AND WATER CHESTNUTS WITH SPAGHETTI

**PREP TIME:** 15 MINUTES
**COOKING TIME:** 10 MINUTES
**SERVES:** 4

¼ cup peanut oil
1 one-inch piece ginger, peeled and minced
4 scallions, thinly sliced (including 2 inches of green)
1 pound pork loin, thinly sliced
1 teaspoon freshly grated orange or tangerine rind
1 teaspoon five-spice powder
¼ cup soy sauce
½ ounce tree ear mushrooms, rehydrated (reserve soaking liquid)
1 (8-ounce) can water chestnuts, drained and sliced
1 tablespoon chopped fresh cilantro
1 pound dried spaghetti, cooked according to package directions

1.  Heat the oil in a wok over high heat. Add the ginger and scallions and stir-fry until aromatic, about 1 or 2 minutes. Add the pork, orange rind, and five-spice powder and stir-fry until the pork is cooked through and no longer pink.

2.  Add the soy sauce, 2 tablespoons of reserved soaking liquid from the mushrooms, the tree ears, and water chestnuts. Stir-fry another minute, or until all ingredients are heated through. Garnish with the fresh cilantro and serve over the cooked spaghetti.

# SPAGHETTI WITH CHICKEN IN SESAME SAUCE

**PREP TIME:** 20 MINUTES
**COOKING TIME:** 10 MINUTES
**SERVES:** 4 TO 6

½ cup toasted sesame paste
¼ cup soy sauce
¼ cup water
½ tablespoon rice vinegar
2 tablespoons peanut oil
1 garlic clove, minced
1 tablespoon minced fresh ginger
3 scallions, thinly sliced (keep the whites and
    the greens separated)
½ pound boneless, skinless chicken breast,
    thinly sliced
1 pound dried spaghetti, cooked according to
    package directions
1 tablespoon toasted sesame oil
½ cup diced celery
½ cup diced cucumber
Chopped fresh cilantro (if desired as a
    garnish)

1. Combine the sesame paste, soy sauce, water, and vinegar in a serving dish large enough to hold the spaghetti.

2. Heat the peanut oil in a wok or 9-inch sauté pan over medium-high heat. Add the garlic, ginger, and the white part of the scallions to the pan and sauté until aromatic, about 1 minute. Add the chicken slices and stir-fry until cooked through and no longer pink, about 5 minutes.

3. When the spaghetti is cooked, drain and toss with the sesame oil. Add the spaghetti to the sesame paste mixture and toss until thoroughly combined. Top with the chicken, celery, cucumber, and the green part of the scallions. Garnish with cilantro, if desired.

## SPAGHETTI WITH SHRIMP

*This dish, as simple as can be, is always a great crowd pleaser, even with young kids. The rock shrimp are sweet and plump and—even better—come already shelled. Serve steamed snow peas on the side.*

**PREP TIME:** 5 MINUTES
**COOKING TIME:** 10 MINUTES
**SERVES:** 4

¼ **cup safflower or canola oil**
4 **scallions, thinly sliced**
1 **one-inch piece fresh ginger, peeled and minced**
2 **garlic cloves, minced**
1¼ **pounds rock shrimp**
1 **pound dried spaghetti, cooked according to package directions**

1. Heat the oil in a wok or deep-sided sauté pan over medium-high heat. When the oil is hot, add the scallions, ginger, and garlic and stir-fry until aromatic, about 1 to 2 minutes.

2. Add the shrimp and stir-fry until shrimp are pink and cooked through, about 3 or 4 minutes. Toss the shrimp mixture with the drained spaghetti.

### VARIATION

SHRIMP IN CURRY OIL: Add 1 tablespoon sweet or hot curry powder to the aromatics and stir-fry 1 or 2 minutes, until dissolved. Top the spaghetti and sauce with 1 cup fresh mung bean sprouts.

## SHRIMP AND VEGETABLES IN COCONUT MILK WITH SPAGHETTI

*Buying shrimp that are already peeled and cleaned will cut the preparation time down to less than 10 minutes. This dish works equally well with chicken. You will find lemongrass in oriental markets if your supermarket doesn't carry it.*

**PREP TIME:** 25 MINUTES
**COOKING TIME:** 12 MINUTES
**SERVES:** 4

¼ cup peanut oil
1 bunch (4 large or 6 small) scallions, thinly sliced (white and 2 inches of green)
1 one-inch piece fresh ginger, peeled and minced
1 stalk lemongrass, thinly sliced
2 garlic cloves, minced
1½ large red bell peppers, seeded and cut into chunks
1 pound medium shrimp, peeled and deveined
1 cup unsweetened coconut milk
1 (8-ounce) can bamboo shoots, drained
Thai fish sauce (nam pla)
2 tablespoons chopped fresh cilantro
1 pound dried spaghetti, cooked according to package directions

1. Heat the oil in a wok over medium-high heat. Add the scallions, ginger, lemongrass, and garlic and stir-fry until aromatic, about 1 to 2 minutes. Add the red bell pepper chunks and stir-fry until softened, 3 to 5 minutes.

2. Add the shrimp and stir-fry 1 minute. Lower the heat slightly. Add the coconut milk and cook, covered, about 3 to 5 minutes longer. Add the bamboo shoots and fish sauce to taste and stir to heat through.

3. Garnish with the cilantro and serve immediately over the cooked spaghetti.

## SPAGHETTI WITH SWEET-AND-SOUR PORK

**PREP TIME:** 10 MINUTES
**COOKING TIME:** 10 MINUTES
**SERVES:** 4

2 tablespoons peanut oil
2 tablespoons minced fresh ginger
3 garlic cloves, minced
1¼ pounds boneless pork loin, thinly sliced
1 onion, chopped (approximately 1¼ cups)
2 small green bell peppers, seeded and cut
    into cubes (approximately 1½ cups)
½ cup tomato ketchup
¼ cup rice vinegar or sake
1 tablespoon sugar
2 teaspoons cornstarch
1 (16-ounce) can pineapple chunks packed in
    juice (reserve the juice)
1 pound dried spaghetti, cooked according to
    package directions
Steamed broccoli (if desired as a garnish)

1. Heat the peanut oil in a wok or deep skillet over high heat. Add the ginger and garlic and stir-fry until aromatic, about 1 to 2 minutes. Add the pork, onion, and green peppers to the wok and stir-fry until the vegetables are softened and the pork is cooked through, about 5 minutes. Add the ketchup and rice vinegar to the mixture. Lower heat to medium and cook 2 or 3 minutes.

2. Dissolve the sugar and cornstarch in ¼ cup of pineapple juice and add to the pork. Toss the ingredients until the sauce thickens and becomes glossy. Add the pineapple chunks and toss until heated through. Serve immediately with the cooked spaghetti. Garnish with broccoli, if desired.

# SPAGHETTI WITH VEGETABLE LO MEIN

*Lo mein are Chinese wheat noodles, but spaghetti makes a fine substitute. You can use any combination of vegetables you like in this recipe, as long as you have a nice balance of textures and colors. Shiitake mushrooms, tofu, carrots, or cabbage would all be delicious.*

**PREP TIME:** 10 MINUTES
**COOKING TIME:** 10 MINUTES
**SERVES:** 4

¼ cup peanut oil
1 one-inch piece ginger, peeled and minced
2 garlic cloves, minced
1 onion, cut into pieces
3 cups bite-sized broccoli florets
1 red bell pepper, seeded and thinly sliced
¼ pound snow peas
⅓ pound white mushrooms, sliced
1 (8-ounce) can water chestnuts, drained
¼ cup soy sauce
2 tablespoons rice wine or dry sherry
1 pound dried spaghetti, cooked according to package directions
2 tablespoons sesame oil

1. Heat the oil in a wok over high heat Add the ginger and garlic and stir-fry until aromatic, 1 to 2 minutes. Add the onion and stir-fry another minute. Add the broccoli florets, red pepper, and snow peas to the wok, stir-frying each a minute or two before adding the next vegetable. Finally, add the mushrooms, water chestnuts, soy sauce, and rice wine and stir-fry another 2 minutes, or until all the vegetables are cooked through.

2. When the spaghetti is cooked, drain and add it to the wok. Toss until combined with the vegetables. Add the sesame oil and toss again. Serve immediately.

## SPAGHETTI IN TERIYAKI SAUCE

*The following is a recipe for homemade teriyaki sauce that you can whip up in minutes. Do not substitute a bottled teriyaki sauce.*

**PREP TIME:** 10 MINUTES
**COOKING TIME:** 10 MINUTES
**SERVES:** 4

1 tablespoon grated fresh ginger
3 garlic cloves, minced
½ cup soy sauce
½ cup water
¼ cup rice wine
2 tablespoons sugar
2 tablespoons honey
1 pound dried spaghetti, cooked according to
    package directions
1 cup grated daikon (white radish)
1 cup grated carrots
8 scallions, cut on the diagonal into 1-inch
    pieces

1. Combine the ginger, garlic, soy sauce, water, rice wine, sugar, and honey in a 1-quart saucepan over medium heat. Swirl the pan occasionally to dissolve the sugar. Bring to a boil and simmer for 2 minutes. Remove from heat and set aside.

2. When the spaghetti is cooked, toss with the teriyaki sauce, daikon, carrots, and scallions. Serve immediately.

# NIFTY FIFTIES

The 1950s were a special time in American history. We had emerged victorious from World War II into an era of booming prosperity and productivity. We had Elvis, Marilyn, Lucy, and Ethel. We liked Ike. But the one thing not quite so renowned was American cuisine.

It was still decades before Julia Child would work her transformation on the eating public with her trailblazing TV program. But many years had passed since America had moved away from its isolationist stance and into the heart of Europe, where, undoubtedly, many a GI Joe had savored the glories of Italian and French cuisine.

I've tried to re-create in this chapter some of the dishes I remember eating when I grew up. They tend to be simplified or Americanized versions of classic European and (given our preoccupation with the "Red Peril") Eastern European dishes. Culinary snobs might dismiss them as "housewife" cuisine. But in my mind, they remain great, nostalgic comfort foods that deserve a special, if transitional, spot in American cooking tradition.

# CHICKEN DIVAN WITH SPAGHETTI

*For a richer-tasting sauce, you can substitute 1 cup chicken (or other) stock for 1 cup of the milk in the white sauce and whisk in 1 or 2 egg yolks with the seasonings after the sauce has thickened.*

**PREP TIME:** 25 MINUTES
**COOKING TIME:** 40 MINUTES
**SERVES:** 4

## WHITE SAUCE

3 tablespoons sweet butter
¼ cup flour
2 cups milk
1 teaspoon tomato paste (optional, for color)
1 teaspoon yellow mustard powder
White pepper, cayenne, nutmeg, and salt

## CHICKEN MIXTURE

1 head broccoli, broken into bite-sized florets
1¼ cups grated sharp yellow Cheddar cheese
4 boneless, skinless chicken breast halves, each cut into 6 pieces
1 pound dried spaghetti, cooked according to package directions

1. To make the sauce, melt the butter in a 2-quart saucepan over medium heat. Add the flour all at once and whisk until thoroughly combined. Continue to cook the flour mixture, whisking, until it begins to bubble and turn golden in color, approximately 3 minutes.

2. Add the milk in a thin stream, whisking constantly, and continue cooking until the sauce thickens. Whisk in the tomato paste (if desired) and season with the mustard powder and white and cayenne peppers, nutmeg, and salt to taste. (The recipe can be prepared several hours ahead up to this point. Cover the surface with plastic wrap and refrigerate until ready to use. Reheat before continuing with the chicken divan.)

3. Preheat the oven to 350 degrees.

4. Cook the broccoli in salted boiling water until crisp-tender. Drain, refresh, and set aside.

5. Heat the white sauce in an ovenproof casserole over medium heat. Add the Cheddar cheese and stir until thoroughly combined. Add the chicken to the sauce and stir to prevent the pieces from sticking together. Bake, covered, in the preheated oven for 25 to 30 minutes, or until the chicken is cooked through.

6. Add the broccoli florets to the chicken mixture and stir until combined. Serve over the cooked spaghetti.

# SPAGHETTI WITH PEPPER STEAK

**PREP TIME:** 10 MINUTES
**COOKING TIME:** 15 MINUTES
**SERVES:** 4

2 tablespoons peanut oil
2 green bell peppers, seeded and thinly sliced (about 2 cups)
1 red bell pepper, seeded and thinly sliced (about 1 cup)
1 onion, thinly sliced
1 pound beef round, thinly sliced
¼ cup soy sauce
1 pound dried spaghetti, cooked according to package directions

1. Heat the oil in a wok or large sauté pan over medium-high heat. Add the red and green bell peppers and onion and cook until the onion is softened and translucent (the peppers should retain some crispness), about 7 or 8 minutes.

2. Turn the heat to high and add the beef slices to the onions and peppers. Sauté until cooked through. Add the soy sauce and cook another minute. Serve over the cooked spaghetti.

## SPAGHETTI WITH CHICKEN CUTLETS PARMIGIANO

*Back in the fifties and sixties this dish was probably more often prepared with veal cutlets, which can be interchangeable with the chicken.*

**PREP TIME:** 10 MINUTES
**COOKING TIME:** 15 MINUTES
**SERVES:** 4

1 cup dry breadcrumbs
⅛ teaspoon EACH garlic powder, salt, and pepper
1 tablespoon grated Romano cheese
½ cup flour
1 egg, lightly beaten with 2 tablespoons water
2 tablespoons olive oil
2 tablespoons safflower oil
1 pound chicken (or veal) cutlets (four ⅛-inch-thick slices)
½ cup Marinara Sauce (page 3) or Classic Italian Tomato Sauce (page 3)
¼ pound mozzarella cheese, grated
1 pound dried spaghetti, cooked according to package directions

1. Combine the breadcrumbs, garlic powder, salt, pepper, and Romano cheese in one shallow dish, put the flour in another, and the beaten egg in a third.

2. Heat the olive oil and safflower oil in a 9-inch skillet over medium-high heat. While the oil is heating, dredge the chicken cutlets in flour. Shake off the excess. Dredge in egg and then in the seasoned breadcrumbs to coat thoroughly.

3. Sauté the chicken cutlets in the hot oil 2 minutes per side, or until golden brown and crispy. Drain on paper towels.

4. Preheat the broiler.

5. Place the chicken cutlets in an ovenproof serving dish. Spoon 1 or 2 tablespoons of marinara or tomato sauce on each and top with a quarter of the mozzarella cheese. Broil for 1 to 2 minutes, or until bubbling and browned. Serve with the cooked spaghetti and additional sauce.

## SPAGHETTI IN VELVEETA® CHEESE SAUCE WITH HOT DOGS

**PREP TIME:** 5 MINUTES
**COOKING TIME:** 10 MINUTES
**SERVES:** 4

½ cup milk
2 tablespoons sweet butter
¾ pound VELVEETA® pasteurized process
    cheese spread
4 small hot dogs (about ⅓ pound ), thinly
    sliced
1 pound dried spaghetti, cooked according to
    package directions

1.  Combine the milk, butter, and cheese in a 1- or 2-quart saucepan over low heat. Cook, stirring occasionally, until the cheese is melted, about 10 minutes.

2.  While the cheese sauce is cooking, sauté the hot dog slices over medium heat until nicely browned and heated through. Remove the hot dog slices with a slotted spoon and add to the cheese sauce.

3. Toss with the cooked spaghetti and serve immediately.

## VARIATIONS

SPAGHETTI VALHALLA: Preheat the broiler. Place the spaghetti and sauce in an ovenproof baking dish. Combine ½ cup breadcrumbs with 2 tablespoons softened sweet butter and 1 teaspoon minced garlic. Top the spaghetti with 12 fresh tomato slices. Place some breadcrumbs on each tomato slice. Run under the broiler 1 or 2 minutes, or until browned.

TUNA NOODLE CASSEROLE: Omit the hot dogs. To the basic recipe add 1½ tablespoons dried, rehydrated onion flakes and 1½ (7-ounce) cans tuna.

MEXICAN-STYLE CHEESE SAUCE: The recipe on the VELVEETA® box suggests you combine 1 cup Mexican-style salsa with 1 pound VELVEETA® pasteurized process cheese spread for a chip dip. You might try adding ½ pound sautéed chorizo or pepperoni sausage to this for a savory spaghetti topping.

## SPAGHETTI ROMANOFF

**PREP TIME:** 5 MINUTES
**COOKING TIME:** 10 MINUTES FOR SPAGHETTI
**SERVES:** 4

2 cups cottage cheese
1 cup sour cream
1 teaspoon ground sweet Hungarian paprika
     (more or less, to taste)
Salt
1 pound dried spaghetti, cooked according to
     package directions
1 cup grated Parmesan cheese

1.  Preheat the broiler.

2.  In an ovenproof serving dish large enough to
hold all the spaghetti, mix together the cottage
cheese, sour cream, and paprika. Season with salt.

3.  Toss the cheese mixture with the cooked
spaghetti until thoroughly combined. Sprinkle the
grated Parmesan on top of the spaghetti. Run the
platter under the broiler until the cheese on top is
browned and bubbling. Serve immediately.

## SPAGHETTI WITH CREAMED CHIPPED BEEF

**PREP TIME:** 15 MINUTES
**COOKING TIME:** 10 MINUTES
**SERVES:** 4

1 recipe White Sauce (page 82) made with 1
     cup beef broth and 1 cup heavy cream
1 cup grated Cheddar cheese
2 tablespoons safflower or canola oil
1 small onion, minced
1¼ pounds ground round or thinly sliced
     round steak
1 pound dried spaghetti, cooked according to
     package directions

1.  Combine the warm white sauce and cheese. Stir
until the cheese melts, and set aside.

2.  Heat the oil in a 9-inch sauté pan over medium
heat. Add the onion and sauté until golden, about 5
minutes. Add the beef and cook, stirring
occasionally, until no longer pink.

3.  Add the sauce to the beef, stir to heat through,
and serve immediately with the cooked spaghetti.

# BEEF GOULASH WITH SPAGHETTI

**PREP TIME:** 15 MINUTES
**COOKING TIME:** 1 HOUR 20 MINUTES
**SERVES:** 4

1½ pounds stewing beef, cut into 1-inch pieces
Flour seasoned with salt and pepper
2 tablespoons safflower or canola oil
1 large onion, sliced
1 small green bell pepper, seeded and
    chopped
1 tablespoon paprika
1 cup beef broth
½ cup dry red wine
1 cup chopped fresh or canned tomatoes
1 garlic clove, minced
1 bay leaf
1 pound dried spaghetti, cooked according to
    package directions

1. Dredge the meat in the flour and shake off any excess.

2. Heat the oil in a 3-quart casserole over medium-high heat. Add the beef to the hot oil, in batches if necessary to prevent crowding, and sauté until browned on all sides. Remove the meat with a slotted spoon and set aside.

3. Lower heat slightly and add the onion and green pepper, stirring to scrape up any browned bits from the bottom of the pan. Sauté the vegetables until softened, about 10 minutes. Add the paprika, stirring constantly for a minute or two. Return the beef to the pan along with the beef broth, wine, tomatoes, garlic, and bay leaf. Lower the heat. Simmer, partially covered, for 1 hour, or until the beef is cooked through. (This can be prepared up to 2 days ahead of time and reheated.)

4. Serve over the cooked spaghetti.

## SWEET-AND-SOUR MEATBALLS WITH SPAGHETTI

*Here's a recipe from our deep, dark culinary past, handed down to my mother and to me by some 1950s sorority sisters whose identity luckily escapes us. (The recipe is printed as it was dictated, but you might want to brown the meatballs in a little oil before proceeding with the sauce making.)*

**PREP TIME:** 10 MINUTES
**COOKING TIME:** 1 HOUR
**SERVES:** 6 TO 8

2 pounds ground beef
4 ounces grape jelly
1 (8-ounce) bottle chili sauce (do not discard
    bottle)
1½ pounds dried spaghetti, cooked according
    to package directions

1. Shape the beef into small meatballs.

2. Melt the grape jelly in a large saucepan or Dutch oven over low heat. Add the chili sauce. Fill the chili sauce bottle a third of the way with water. Shake well and add this to the sauce. Taste for seasoning.

3. Add the meatballs and simmer over low heat until cooked through, about an hour. Serve with the cooked spaghetti.

# SPAGHETTI WITH "SLOPPY JOE" SAUCE

*Sloppy Joes, a recipe typifying 1960s American cuisine, was one of the first dishes I learned to cook (along with tuna melts and Halloween cupcakes) at a class given by the local YMCA. It is re-created here as a quick and easy spaghetti topping you can prepare in minutes.*

**PREP TIME:** 5 MINUTES
**COOKING TIME:** 10 MINUTES
**SERVES:** 4

1½ tablespoons safflower or canola oil
1 small onion, minced
1 pound ground beef, broken up with a
    spatula
1 garlic clove, minced
1 cup puréed or crushed tomatoes
Salt and pepper to taste
1 pound dried spaghetti, cooked according to
    package directions

1. Heat the oil in a 9-inch sauté pan over medium heat. Add the onion and sauté until soft and translucent, about 5 minutes. Add the beef and garlic and sauté until beef is cooked through. Drain excess fat from the pan.

2. Add the tomatoes and salt and pepper to taste. Cook until heated through. Serve over cooked spaghetti.

## VARIATION

SPAGHETTI WITH CHILI SAUCE: Add ¼ teaspoon oregano, ¾ teaspoon EACH ground cumin and ground chili powder, ⅛ teaspoon cayenne (more or less to taste), and 1 (16-ounce) can kidney beans to the Sloppy Joe sauce with the tomatoes.

## MEATBALLS STROGANOFF OVER SPAGHETTI

*I like to use a combination of different meats—it produces a lighter, more interesting texture in the meatballs. If you prefer, substitute 1 pound ground beef and omit the Swiss chard from the recipe.*

**PREP TIME:** 25 MINUTES
**COOKING TIME:** 1 HOUR 20 MINUTES
**SERVES:** 4

¾ pound Swiss chard, stemmed and rinsed
1 tablespoon freshly squeezed lemon juice
½ pound ground pork
½ pound ground veal
1 large onion, finely minced (about ¾ cup)
1 large egg
⅓ cup dry breadcrumbs
2 tablespoons grated Parmesan cheese
1 teaspoon salt
⅛ teaspoon black pepper
⅛ teaspoon grated nutmeg
¼ cup vegetable oil
2 cups pork, veal, or beef stock
2 tablespoons sweet butter
1 (12-ounce) package mushrooms, stemmed and sliced
1 tablespoon vermouth
2 tablespoons cornstarch
1 cup sour cream
1 pound dried spaghetti, cooked according to package directions

## FOR THE MEATBALLS

1. Drop the chard leaves into a large saucepan containing 2 inches of salted boiling water mixed with the lemon juice. Cook approximately 3 to 5 minutes, or until the leaves are wilted but still slightly chewy. Drain and run the chard under very cold water. Squeeze out as much excess liquid as possible and chop it fine.

2. Mix ½ cup of the chopped chard with the pork, veal, ½ cup of onion, the egg, breadcrumbs, cheese, salt, pepper, and nutmeg. Combine thoroughly but do not overmix. Using a ⅛-cup measure, form the meat into small balls.

3. Heat the oil in a 9-inch sauté pan over high heat. Sauté the meatballs, in batches if necessary to prevent crowding. When they are nicely browned on all sides, remove the meatballs and drain on paper towels.

## FOR THE SAUCE

4. Bring the stock to a boil in a 3½-quart Dutch oven or other heavy pot large enough to accommodate the meatballs. Add the meatballs.

Reduce the heat to a simmer and cook, covered, for 1 hour. When the meatballs are cooked, remove them from the stock and keep warm.

5. While the meatballs are cooking, melt the butter in a sauté pan over medium heat. Add the remaining ¼ cup of onion and sauté until golden and translucent, about 5 minutes. Add the sliced mushrooms and cook until they give up their liquid. Add the vermouth, turn the heat to high, and boil the mushroom mixture for 1 or 2 minutes. Remove the pan from the heat, remove the mushrooms with a slotted spoon, and set them aside.

6. To finish the dish: Stir ¼ cup of the hot stock into the cornstarch until dissolved. Whisk the cornstarch and sour cream into the stock and cook over low heat until thickened. Add the mushrooms and meatballs to the sauce and cook over very low heat until heated through. Taste and adjust for seasoning. Serve immediately over the cooked spaghetti.

# FROM THE BACK OF THE BOX

This chapter features recipes from America's two largest—and, I'm told, most competitive—national pasta manufacturers. Developed or tested by home economists under the auspices of the Borden and Hershey Foods corporate test kitchens, the recipes cover a wide range of flavors and styles and are reprinted here.

Many of the recipes suggest that one pound of pasta yields eight servings. Since most people I know tend to cook up practically an entire box of spaghetti to serve just two, this seems a bit conservative to me. However, the sauces are pretty substantial and chock-full of ingredients. You might just want to adjust the serving sizes according to the appetites and relative enthusiasm or self-restraint of your family and friends.

# BARBECUED MEATBALLS AND SPAGHETTI

**PREP TIME:** 20 MINUTES
**COOKING TIME:** 40 MINUTES
**SERVES:** 4

1 pound ground beef
2 tablespoons finely chopped onion
1 teaspoon salt, divided
¼ teaspoon ground black pepper
2 tablespoons vegetable oil
1 (10¾-ounce) can condensed tomato soup
1 cup water
¼ cup sweet pickle relish
2 tablespoons vinegar
2 tablespoons ketchup
1 tablespoon brown sugar
½ package (8 ounces) *San Giorgio* Spaghetti,
   uncooked

1. In a medium bowl, combine the meat, onion, ½ teaspoon salt, and the pepper; form into 1-inch balls.

2. In a large skillet, heat the oil. Brown meatballs until almost done; drain off fat. Blend in soup, water, pickle relish, vinegar, ketchup, brown sugar, and remaining salt. Heat to boiling; reduce heat. Simmer, uncovered, 25 minutes, or until thickened.

3. Meanwhile, cook the pasta according to package directions; drain. Toss the hot pasta with meatballs and sauce.

# CHICKEN AND SPAGHETTI PIE

**PREP TIME:** 10 MINUTES
**COOKING TIME:** 30 MINUTES
**SERVES:** 4 TO 6

½ package (8 ounces) *American Beauty*
   Spaghetti, uncooked
2 chicken breasts, skinned and boned (about
   1½ pounds)
1 tablespoon vegetable oil
¼ cup (½ stick) butter or margarine
¼ cup all-purpose flour
½ teaspoon salt
½ teaspoon ground black pepper
1 cup chicken broth
½ cup whipping cream
2 tablespoons dry sherry
½ cup grated Parmesan cheese

1. Cook the pasta according to package directions; drain.

2. Cut the chicken into 1-inch pieces. In a large skillet over medium heat, heat the oil; add chicken. Cook 5 minutes, or until pink disappears, stirring frequently.

3. Heat the oven to 350 degrees.

4. In a large saucepan, melt the butter; stir in the flour and seasonings. Cook over low heat 1 minute; stir in chicken broth and whipping cream. Heat to boiling, stirring frequently. Stir in the sherry, spaghetti, and chicken; spoon into a 2-quart casserole. Sprinkle with cheese. Bake 15 to 20 minutes, or until bubbly.

# LAYERED MARINARA BAKE

**PREP TIME:** 20 MINUTES
**COOKING TIME:** 45 MINUTES
**SERVES:** 8 TO 10

2 tablespoons olive or vegetable oil
½ cup chopped onion
2 garlic cloves, minced
3½ cups (28-ounce can) whole tomatoes, undrained and chopped
1¾ cups (15-ounce can) tomato sauce
2 tablespoons chopped fresh parsley
2 teaspoons dried basil leaves
1 teaspoon sugar
Salt and pepper
1 package (16 ounces) *Ronzoni* Spaghetti Twists, uncooked
3 cups sliced zucchini
2 cups (8 ounces) shredded mozzarella cheese, divided

1. Heat the oven to 350 degrees.

2. In a 3-quart saucepan, heat the oil. Add the onion and garlic; cook until tender. Stir in the tomatoes with liquid, tomato sauce, parsley, basil leaves, and seasonings; heat to boiling. Reduce heat; cook 15 minutes, or until thickened.

3. Meanwhile, cook the pasta according to package directions; drain. Toss the hot pasta with the zucchini and sauce. In a 3-quart baking dish, place half the pasta mixture; sprinkle with 1 cup of the cheese. Top with remaining pasta mixture; sprinkle with the remaining cheese. Bake 25 to 30 minutes, or until hot and bubbly.

# QUICK AND EASY CACCIATORE

**PREP TIME:** 15 MINUTES
**COOKING TIME:** 30 MINUTES
**SERVES:** 6 TO 8

3 tablespoons olive or vegetable oil, divided
1½ cups sliced onion
1½ cups (about 5 ounces) fresh mushrooms
1 cup coarsely chopped green pepper
2 garlic cloves, minced
1½ pounds boneless, skinless chicken breasts
1 package (16 ounces) *Skinner* Spaghetti,
    uncooked
3 cups (30-ounce jar) spaghetti sauce
Salt and pepper
Grated Parmesan cheese

1. In a large skillet, heat 2 tablespoons oil. Add the onion, mushrooms, green pepper, and garlic; cook over medium-high heat 5 minutes, or until tender. Remove the vegetables; set aside. Add the remaining oil to the skillet; cook chicken 8 minutes on each side, or until the pink disappears.

2. Meanwhile, cook the pasta according to package directions; drain. Add the spaghetti sauce and vegetables to chicken. Cook 5 minutes, or until sauce is heated through. Add salt and pepper to taste.

3. Place the pasta on a serving platter; arrange chicken pieces on top. Pour sauce over pasta and chicken; serve with Parmesan cheese.

# SECOND WIND SHRIMP & VEGGIE PASTA

**PREP TIME:** 30 MINUTES
**COOKING TIME:** 10 MINUTES
**SERVES:** 4 TO 6

½ package (8 ounces) *Ronzoni* Linguine or
    Thin Spaghetti, uncooked
1½ cups chicken broth
1½ cups chopped onion
1 cup sliced carrot
6 garlic cloves, minced
½ teaspoon salt
½ teaspoon ground black pepper
1 pound medium fresh shrimp, peeled and
    deveined
4 cups fresh broccoli florets
1½ cups diced sweet red pepper
¼ cup chopped fresh dill or 2 teaspoons
    dried dill weed
2 teaspoons Worcestershire sauce
⅔ cup grated Parmesan cheese

1. Cook the pasta according to package directions; drain.

2. Meanwhile, in a large skillet, heat the broth to boiling; add the onion, carrot, garlic, salt, and pepper. Reduce heat; simmer 5 minutes. Add the shrimp, broccoli, and red pepper; heat to boiling. Reduce heat; simmer 3 minutes, or until shrimp turn pink and broccoli is crisp-tender. Stir in dill and Worcestershire sauce.

3. Place hot pasta on a large platter; sprinkle with half the cheese. Top with the shrimp mixture and remaining cheese.

# CELEBRATION SPAGHETTI

**PREP TIME:** 20 MINUTES
**COOKING TIME:** 25 MINUTES
**SERVES:** 6 TO 8

1 tablespoon olive oil
2 medium zucchini, sliced
2 cups sliced fresh mushrooms
1 medium green bell pepper, cut into thin
    strips
1 (28-ounce) can whole tomatoes, cut up
    (undrained)
2 (6-ounce) cans tomato paste
1 cup sliced pitted ripe olives
1 teaspoon salt
½ teaspoon basil leaves
¼ teaspoon pepper
¼ cup grated Parmesan cheese
1 (1-pound) package Creamette® Thin
    Spaghetti, uncooked
2 tablespoons softened margarine or butter
Grated Parmesan cheese

1. In a large skillet, heat the oil. Add the zucchini, mushrooms, and green pepper; cook until crisp-tender. Stir in tomatoes, tomato paste, olives, salt, basil, and pepper. Bring to a boil. Reduce heat; simmer 15 minutes. Stir in the Parmesan cheese.

2. Prepare the Creamette Thin Spaghetti according to package directions; drain. Toss with the softened margarine. Arrange on a warm platter. Top with the vegetable mixture and Parmesan cheese. Serve immediately. Refrigerate leftovers.

# SPAGHETTI MILANO

**PREP TIME:** 15 MINUTES
**COOKING TIME:** 20 MINUTES
**SERVES:** 6 TO 8

1 pound bulk sausage or ground beef
1 cup chopped onion
½ cup chopped green bell pepper
1 medium carrot, finely chopped
1 garlic clove, minced
2 (15-ounce) cans tomato sauce
1 (6-ounce) can tomato paste
1 (6½-ounce) can minced clams, undrained
1 (4-ounce) can mushroom stems and pieces,
    drained
1 teaspoon salt
½ teaspoon pepper
½ teaspoon basil leaves
¼ teaspoon thyme leaves
1 (1-pound) package Creamette® Thin
    Spaghetti, uncooked
3 tablespoons softened margarine or butter
Grated Parmesan cheese

1. In a medium skillet, cook the sausage, onion, green pepper, carrot, and garlic until the sausage is no longer pink and the carrot is tender; drain. Add the tomato sauce, tomato paste, clams and their juice, mushrooms, salt, pepper, basil, and thyme. Bring to a boil. Reduce heat; simmer 20 minutes.

2. Prepare Creamette Thin Spaghetti according to package directions; drain. Toss with softened margarine. Serve the sauce over the hot spaghetti; top with Parmesan cheese. Refrigerate leftovers.

## SPAGHETTI WITH TURKEY MEATBALLS

**PREP TIME:** 5 MINUTES
**COOKING TIME:** 30 MINUTES
**SERVES:** 8 TO 10

1½ pounds fresh ground turkey or chicken
½ cup dry Italian breadcrumbs
1 egg
1 tablespoon Wyler's® or Steero® Chicken-
    Flavor Instant Bouillon
2 teaspoons Italian seasoning
Freshly ground pepper
2 tablespoons vegetable oil
2 (26-ounce) jars Classico® di Roma
    Arrabbiata (Spicy Red Pepper) Pasta
    Sauce
1 (1-pound) package Creamette® Spaghetti,
    uncooked
Grated Parmesan cheese

1. In a bowl, combine the turkey, crumbs, egg, bouillon, Italian seasoning, and pepper; mix well. Shape into 1¼-inch meatballs.

2. In a Dutch oven over medium heat, brown the meatballs in oil. Add the pasta sauce; mix well. Bring to a boil; reduce heat and simmer 20 to 30 minutes.

3. Prepare the spaghetti as the package directs. Serve the meatballs and sauce over spaghetti with Parmesan cheese. Refrigerate leftovers.

# QUICKIE SPAGHETTI

These are recipes perfect for those days when you don't have the time or energy to make anything complicated. The sauces are simple, adaptable, and easy to prepare—some require minimum cooking while others are no-cook sauces and toppings especially appropriate for warmer weather. With the addition of a few ingredients, they can also be dressed up for a more festive presentation. To make things even easier, virtually all the recipes call for ingredients that most people have sitting around in their refrigerators or pantries on a regular basis: herbs and spices, butter, oil, cheese, eggs, canned goods, prepared appetizers, and condiments like ketchup, mayonnaise, and barbecue sauce.

## BUTTER SAUCES

*These are elegant and unbelievably simple sauces to prepare, especially since almost everybody always has a couple of sticks of butter in the refrigerator. They are quite rich, however. So, if you prefer, you can use half margarine and half butter instead, or even replace a few tablespoons of butter with canola or safflower oil. Each recipe makes enough for 1 pound of spaghetti.*

## GREEN HERB BUTTER

*You can try this with other herbs or seasonal greens (for example, dandelion greens or sorrel instead of the watercress, or chervil, chives, sage, or rosemary in place of the parsley and tarragon) if you wish.*

**PREP TIME:** 5 MINUTES
**COOKING TIME:** 5 MINUTES
**SERVES:** 4

½ **bunch watercress, washed and tough stems removed**
3 **sprigs fresh tarragon**
3 **sprigs fresh parsley**
¼ **pound (1 stick) sweet butter, melted**
**Freshly squeezed lemon juice**
**Salt and pepper**

Place the watercress, tarragon, and parsley in the container of a food processor or blender and pulse until finely chopped. Measure out ½ cup of chopped herbs and add to the melted butter. Season with lemon juice and salt and pepper to taste.

# SPAGHETTI WITH LEMON BUTTER

**PREP TIME:** 5 MINUTES
**COOKING TIME:** 10 MINUTES
**SERVES:** 4

2 tablespoons freshly squeezed lemon juice
2 teaspoons grated lemon zest
1½ tablespoons chopped fresh parsley
Salt and freshly ground black pepper
¼ pound (1 stick) sweet butter, melted
1 pound dried spaghetti, cooked according to
    package directions

1. Add the lemon juice, lemon zest, parsley, salt, and pepper to taste to the melted butter.

2. Toss with the cooked spaghetti and serve immediately.

## VARIATIONS

LEMON SHALLOT BUTTER: Sauté ½ cup minced shallots in the butter as it melts. Combine with the remaining ingredients and toss with spaghetti.

LEMON GARLIC BUTTER: Add 2 tablespoons minced garlic to the melted butter along with the remaining ingredients and toss with spaghetti.

LEMON AND BLACK PEPPER BUTTER: Use 1½ tablespoons freshly ground black pepper and proceed with the recipe.

## SPAGHETTI WITH POPPY SEED AND ALMOND BUTTER

**PREP TIME:** 5 MINUTES
**COOKING TIME:** 10 MINUTES
**SERVES:** 4

¼ pound (1 stick) sweet butter
½ cup blanched, sliced almonds
2 tablespoons poppy seeds
Freshly squeezed lemon juice
Salt and pepper
1 pound dried spaghetti, cooked according to
    package directions

1.  Melt the butter in a 9-inch sauté pan. Add the almonds and sauté until they become lightly toasted. Add the poppy seeds and lemon juice to taste. Season with salt and pepper.

2.  Toss the cooked spaghetti in the almond-poppy butter and serve immediately.

## OIL-BASED SAUCES

*Like butter sauces, these are quick and easy to prepare. However, because oil has a higher burning point than butter and is more neutral in taste, it can be combined more harmoniously with spicier, highly flavored ingredients. Following are a few suggestions making the most of our favorite international cuisines. Any of these would be delicious with shrimp or chicken (approximately 1 pound of cleaned shrimp or sliced chicken) sautéed in the hot oil. These will all make enough for a pound of spaghetti.*

# SPAGHETTI WITH INDIA OIL

**PREP TIME:** 5 MINUTES
**COOKING TIME:** 10 MINUTES
**SERVES:** 4

½ cup peanut oil
1½ teaspoons fenugreek
1½ teaspoons EACH coriander, cumin, and
   yellow mustard seeds
1 pound dried spaghetti, cooked according to
   package directions

Salt

1. Heat ½ cup peanut oil in a wok or sauté pan. Add the fenugreek, coriander, cumin, and yellow mustard seeds and sauté 1 or 2 minutes, or until the seeds begin to brown and pop. Be careful not to burn the seeds.

2. Toss the oil with the cooked spaghetti. Season with salt to taste and serve immediately.

# SPAGHETTI WITH CHILI-LIME OIL

**PREP TIME:** 10 MINUTES
**COOKING TIME:** 10 MINUTES
**SERVES:** 4

½ cup peanut oil
2 tablespoons chili powder
2 tablespoons fresh lime juice
1 teaspoon grated lime zest
1 pound dried spaghetti, cooked according to
   package directions

Salt

1. Heat the peanut oil in a wok or sauté pan. Add the chili powder and sauté 1 to 2 minutes, or until the chili powder starts to brown lightly. Be careful not to burn it. Add the lime juice and lime zest to the oil.

2. Toss with the cooked spaghetti. Season with salt and serve immediately.

# ORIENTAL OIL

**PREP TIME:** 5 MINUTES
**COOKING TIME:** 10 MINUTES
**SERVES:** 4

½ cup peanut oil
1 one-inch piece fresh ginger, peeled and
    minced
1 bunch scallions (white only), thinly sliced
2 or 3 garlic cloves, minced
1 pound dried spaghetti, cooked according to
    package directions

Heat the oil in a wok or sauté pan over high heat.
Add the ginger, scallions, and garlic and sauté until
aromatic, about 1 to 2 minutes. Serve with
spaghetti.

## VARIATIONS

CHINESE FIVE-SPICE OIL: Add 1 tablespoon five-
spice powder to the oil and vegetables. Sauté an
additional 1 to 2 minutes and serve with cooked
spaghetti.

CURRY OIL: Add 2 tablespoons sweet or hot curry
powder to the oil and vegetables. Sauté an
additional 1 to 2 minutes and serve with cooked
spaghetti.

HOT OIL: Add 1 teaspoon red pepper flakes to the
oil and vegetables and serve with cooked spaghetti.

ORANGE HOT OIL: Add 2 teaspoons grated
orange (or tangerine) zest and 1 teaspoon hot
pepper flakes to the hot oil. Cook 1 to 2 minutes,
being careful not to burn the orange rind. Serve
with cooked spaghetti.

# CHEESE SAUCES FOR SPAGHETTI

*Tossing fresh cheese with hot pasta can create some of the easiest and most satisfying dishes possible. Following are several fuss-free examples you can prepare in no time. Adding an egg to the cheese mixture will make it creamier and easier to toss with the cooked spaghetti. However, if you are afraid of eating undercooked or raw egg products because of possible contamination with salmonella, you can easily leave them out.*

## SPAGHETTI WITH FOUR CHEESES

*Feel free to substitute other cheeses for the fontina and Gorgonzola suggested below. I like to serve this topped with tomato sauce to cut down on the richness of the dish.*

**PREP TIME:** 10 MINUTES
**COOKING TIME:** 10 MINUTES FOR SPAGHETTI
**SERVES:** 6

½ pound mozzarella cheese, shredded
1 cup ricotta cheese
¼ pound semisoft Italian cheese, such as
    fontina or caciocavallo
2 ounces Gorgonzola cheese
1 egg, lightly beaten (optional)
Salt, white pepper, and nutmeg
1 pound dried spaghetti, cooked according to
    package directions

1. Combine the cheeses and egg, if desired, in a serving dish large enough to hold the spaghetti. Season with salt, white pepper, and nutmeg to taste.

2. Toss with the hot spaghetti until the cheese is melted and thoroughly combined. Serve immediately.

## SPAGHETTI WITH CREAMY PARMESAN SAUCE

**PREP TIME:** 5 MINUTES
**COOKING TIME:** 10 MINUTES FOR SPAGHETTI
**SERVES:** 4

1½ cups ricotta cheese
1 cup grated Parmesan cheese
½ cup grated Romano cheese
1 egg, lightly beaten (optional)
Salt, freshly ground white pepper, and nutmeg
1 pound dried spaghetti, cooked according to
    package directions

1. In a serving dish large enough to hold the spaghetti, combine the ricotta, Parmesan, and Romano cheeses and the egg, if desired. Season with salt, white pepper, and nutmeg to taste.

2. Toss with the hot cooked spaghetti until thoroughly combined. Serve immediately.

## SPAGHETTI WITH BLUE CHEESE AND WALNUTS

*Before preparing this dish, taste your blue cheese to gauge its pungency. If it's a really strong-tasting or piquant blue, you might wish to substitute cream cheese or mascarpone for some of the blue cheese.*

**PREP TIME:** 5 MINUTES
**COOKING TIME:** 10 MINUTES FOR SPAGHETTI
**SERVES:** 4

⅔ cup crumbled blue cheese (about ½ pound)
4 scallions, thinly sliced
½ cup chopped walnuts
¼ cup light cream or milk
Salt and freshly ground black pepper
1 pound dried spaghetti, cooked according to
    package directions

1. Combine the blue cheese, scallions, walnuts, and cream in a bowl large enough to hold the cooked spaghetti. Season with salt and pepper if desired.

2. Toss with the hot cooked spaghetti. Serve immediately.

## SPAGHETTI WITH COTTAGE CHEESE AND SUMMER VEGETABLES

**PREP TIME:** 15 MINUTES
**COOKING TIME:** 10 MINUTES FOR SPAGHETTI
**SERVES:** 4

2 cups cottage cheese
½ cup sour cream
1 cup chopped tomatoes
½ large cucumber, seeded and diced
½ cup sliced radishes
3 scallions, thinly sliced
1 pound dried spaghetti, cooked according to
    package directions

1.  Combine all ingredients (except the spaghetti) in a large serving bowl.

2.  When the spaghetti is cooked, drain and refresh it with cold water. Toss the spaghetti with the cottage cheese mixture and serve immediately, at room temperature.

## SPAGHETTI WITH CELERY, GREEN OLIVES, AND CREAM CHEESE

**PREP TIME:** 10 MINUTES
**COOKING TIME:** 10 MINUTES FOR SPAGHETTI
**SERVES:** 4

2 large celery stalks, minced (about 1 cup)
4 ounces (drained weight) pimiento-stuffed
    green olives, chopped (about 1 cup)
1 small garlic clove, minced
4 ounces cream cheese, at room temperature
2 to 4 tablespoons milk or cream
1 pound dried spaghetti, cooked according to
    package directions

1.  Combine the celery, olives, garlic, and cream cheese in a serving bowl large enough to hold the cooked spaghetti. Add the milk or cream a tablespoon at a time to thin the mixture to the consistency you prefer.

2.  Toss with the hot cooked spaghetti and serve immediately.

## SPAGHETTI CARBONARA

*Here is a classic Italian dish requiring virtually no cooking or preparation. However, it does use raw eggs, which become partially cooked when tossed with the hot spaghetti. If you are concerned about the possibility of getting salmonella from eating undercooked eggs or poultry products, this is probably not the dish for you.*

**PREP TIME:** 5 MINUTES
**COOKING TIME:** 10 MINUTES
**SERVES:** 4

2 tablespoons sweet butter
¼ pound pancetta, cut into ¼-inch cubes
3 extra-large eggs
1 teaspoon freshly ground black pepper
Salt
Freshly grated nutmeg
1 pound dried spaghetti, cooked according to
    package directions
1½ cups grated Parmesan cheese

1. Melt the butter in a 5-inch sauté pan over medium heat. Add the pancetta and cook until golden. Remove from the heat.

2. In a serving dish large enough to hold the spaghetti, lightly beat the eggs. Season with the pepper, salt, and nutmeg. When the spaghetti is cooked, drain and quickly toss with the egg mixture until the eggs begin to "cook" and thicken. Add the pancetta mixture and the Parmesan cheese. Taste for salt and adjust seasoning. Serve immediately.

# BASIC CREAM SAUCE

*A few years back, it would have been unthinkable to include a recipe using this much heavy cream (and cheese!). Daily news reports bombarded us with propaganda about good cholesterol, bad cholesterol, lipids, triglycerides, saturated fat, unsaturated fat, hydrogenated fat. The food police were watching at every doughnut counter and fast-food restaurant. However, the tide has turned. Refugees of the fat wars are eating bacon and double cheeseburgers again. Indulgence is in. So here's a recipe for all those who suffered through years of "spa cuisine" and fat deprivation. It's easy to make, cooks in minutes, and can be dressed up or down to suit any mood, flavor, or occasion. The possibilities are limited only by your imagination. The basic recipe is followed by several variations.*

**PREP TIME:** 5 MINUTES
**COOKING TIME:** 15 MINUTES
**SERVES:** 4

2 tablespoons sweet butter
4 shallots, minced
¼ cup dry white wine
1½ cups heavy cream
Freshly grated nutmeg
Salt and white pepper
1 pound dried spaghetti, cooked according to
    package directions
4 ounces grated Parmesan cheese

1. Melt the butter in a sauté pan over medium heat. Add the shallots and sauté until golden and translucent, about 2 or 3 minutes.

2. Turn the heat to high and add the wine and cream. Reduce the cream until thick enough to coat the back of a spoon, approximately 10 minutes. Season with nutmeg, salt, and pepper to taste.

3. Drain the spaghetti and toss with the cream mixture and Parmesan cheese. Serve immediately.

## VARIATIONS

**SMOKED SALMON AND HERB CREAM SAUCE:** To the reduced cream add ¼ pound smoked salmon, cut into thin strips, and 3 tablespoons minced fresh tarragon or dill.

**PROSCIUTTO AND PEAS:** To the reduced cream add 2 ounces shredded prosciutto and 1 cup cooked peas.

**TOMATO CREAM SAUCE:** Add 1½ teaspoons tomato paste and 1 cup chopped fresh tomatoes to the cream and reduce as directed.

**HERB CREAM SAUCE:** Add 3 or 4 tablespoons minced fresh herbs or a combination, such as rosemary, sage, basil, thyme, marjoram, and the like, to the reduced cream.

**CURRY CREAM SAUCE:** Add 1½ tablespoons curry powder to the cooked shallots and sauté 1 or 2 minutes. Proceed with the recipe, but omit the Parmesan cheese. You might try adding seafood, such as 1½ cups cooked baby shrimp, 1 (4-ounce) can smoked mussels, or 1 pound bay scallops sautéed in 2 tablespoons butter.

**SAFFRON CREAM SAUCE:** Dissolve 1 teaspoon saffron threads in 1 tablespoon hot water. Add to the cream and reduce as directed. You could also add the same types and amounts of seafood as suggested for curry cream sauce.

**CAJUN CREAM SAUCE:** Add 1½ tablespoons Cajun Spice mixture (page 24) to the cooked shallots and sauté 1 or 2 minutes. Proceed with the recipe. You might try adding 2 ounces diced tasso (spicy Cajun ham) and 1½ cups cooked baby shrimp to the sauce.

## SPAGHETTI WITH OLIVE OIL AND GARLIC

**PREP TIME:** 5 MINUTES
**COOKING TIME:** 5 MINUTES
**SERVES:** 4

¾ cup good quality olive oil
6 garlic cloves, thinly sliced (more or less, to
  taste)
1½ teaspoons salt
1 teaspoon freshly squeezed lemon juice
2 tablespoons dry white wine
1 pound dried spaghetti, cooked according to
  package directions

1.  Heat the olive oil in a sauté pan over medium-high heat. Add the garlic to the hot oil and cook it until lightly browned. Be careful not to burn it.

2.  Lower the heat and add the salt, lemon juice, and wine. Cook for 1 or 2 minutes longer. Toss with the hot spaghetti and serve immediately.

*Following are three easy-to-prepare cold spaghetti salads with mayonnaise-based sauces. Their flavor really improves when they are refrigerated several hours, preferably overnight.*

## SPAGHETTI SALAD

**PREP TIME:** 10 MINUTES
**COOKING TIME:** 10 MINUTES FOR SPAGHETTI
**SERVES:** 6 TO 8

1 cup mayonnaise
2 tablespoons sugar
1 tablespoon freshly squeezed lemon juice or
  white vinegar
1½ teaspoons salt
1 teaspoon paprika
1 teaspoon celery seed
Freshly ground black pepper
1 large carrot, grated
1 green bell pepper, seeded and grated
2 tablespoons grated onion
1 pound dried spaghetti, cooked according to
  package directions

(continued on next page)

1. Combine the mayonnaise, sugar, lemon juice, salt, paprika, and celery seed in a mixing bowl large enough to hold the spaghetti. Taste and adjust for seasoning. (You want a balance among the sweet, sour, and salty elements.) Season with ground black pepper to taste. Add the carrot, green pepper, and onion to the sauce.

2. When the spaghetti is cooked, drain and refresh briefly with cold water. Toss with the dressing and chill until ready to use.

## SPAGHETTI WITH SAUCE RÉMOULADE

**PREP TIME:** 5 MINUTES
**COOKING TIME:** 10 MINUTES FOR SPAGHETTI
**SERVES:** 6 TO 8

1 cup mayonnaise
1 tablespoon minced onion
1½ tablespoons capers
2 tablespoons chopped cornichons
1 teaspoon dried tarragon OR 1 tablespoon fresh
1 tablespoon minced fresh parsley
1 teaspoon freshly squeezed lemon juice
Salt and pepper
1 pound dried spaghetti, cooked according to package directions

1. Combine all ingredients (except the spaghetti) in a bowl. Taste and adjust for seasoning.

2. When the spaghetti is cooked, drain and refresh briefly with cold water. Toss with the dressing and chill until ready to use.

## RUSSIAN SPAGHETTI SALAD

**PREP TIME:** 25 MINUTES
**COOKING TIME:** 10 MINUTES FOR SPAGHETTI
**SERVES:** 6 TO 8

1 cup mayonnaise
⅓ cup ketchup
2 tablespoons finely minced onion
1 teaspoon sweet paprika
Salt and freshly ground black pepper
1 pound dried spaghetti, cooked according to
    package directions
1 cup cooked cubed ham
1 cup cooked cubed turkey
2 hard-cooked eggs, cut into eighths

1. Combine the mayonnaise, ketchup, onion, and paprika in a mixing bowl large enough to hold the spaghetti. Season with salt and pepper to taste.

2. When the spaghetti is cooked, drain and refresh briefly in cold water. Toss with the dressing, ham, and turkey. Top with the hard-cooked eggs.

## SPAGHETTI AND BROCCOLI SALAD

*The broccoli mixture tastes better when allowed to marinate for several hours, preferably overnight, in the refrigerator.*

**PREP TIME:** 10 MINUTES
**COOKING TIME:** 10 MINUTES FOR SPAGHETTI
**SERVES:** 4

2 heads broccoli, cut into bite-sized florets
1 tablespoon rice wine vinegar
1½ teaspoons prepared mustard
2 tablespoons soy sauce
1 garlic clove, minced
½ cup safflower oil
1 pound dried spaghetti, cooked according to
    package directions

1. Bring a few inches of salted water to a boil in a 4-quart saucepan Add the broccoli florets and blanch 2 or 3 minutes, or until crisp-tender. Drain and refresh with cold water.

(continued on next page)

2. In a serving dish large enough to hold the broccoli, combine the vinegar, mustard, soy sauce, and garlic. Whisk until combined. Gradually whisk in the oil until incorporated into a thick sauce. Toss with the broccoli.

3. When the spaghetti is cooked, drain and refresh briefly with cold water. Toss with the broccoli mixture and serve immediately at room temperature.

*Following are three recipes for classic French-Mediterranean sauces—anchoiade (anchovy sauce); tapenade (black olive), and the well-known pistou, more commonly known as pesto. The recipes make 1 cup of sauce, enough for 1 pound of spaghetti. You can try adding a can of tuna to either the anchovy or olive sauces for a change of pace. Goat cheese (1 ounce per person) is also delicious with the tapenade.*

## SPAGHETTI WITH ANCHOVY SAUCE

**PREP TIME:** 5 MINUTES
**COOKING TIME:** 10 MINUTES FOR SPAGHETTI
**SERVES:** 4

**10 anchovy fillets, drained and patted dry
1 garlic clove
2 tablespoons Italian parsley leaves
1½ teaspoons balsamic vinegar
1½ teaspoons freshly squeezed lemon juice
½ teaspoon EACH dried thyme and basil
½ cup fresh breadcrumbs
¼ cup olive oil
1 pound dried spaghetti, cooked according to package directions**

1. Place the anchovies, garlic, parsley, vinegar, lemon juice, and herbs in the container of a blender or food processor. Pulse until finely chopped, scraping down sides of workbowl as necessary. Add the breadcrumbs and pulse to combine.

2. With the motor running, add the olive oil in a thin stream until the sauce is nicely thickened and emulsified.

3. Serve over hot cooked spaghetti.

# TAPENADE FOR SPAGHETTI

**PREP TIME:** 5 MINUTES
**COOKING TIME:** 10 MINUTES FOR SPAGHETTI
**SERVES:** 4

**1 cup pitted black olives**
**1 tablespoon capers**
**1 garlic clove**
**2 anchovy fillets**
**½ tablespoon freshly squeezed lemon juice**
**6 tablespoons olive oil**
**1 pound dried spaghetti, cooked according to package directions**

1. Place the olives, capers, garlic, and anchovies in the container of a blender or food processor. Add the lemon juice and pulse gently to combine.

2. With the motor running, drizzle the olive oil into the olive mixture a tablespoon at a time until the mixture is thickened and emulsified.

3. Serve over hot cooked spaghetti.

## PESTO SAUCE FOR SPAGHETTI

*Pesto, like salsa, was one of the great sauce phenomena of the 1980s. At this point, it is so well known that it seems to be used almost as commonly, and in much the same ways, as mayonnaise. I've included it here because, despite its ubiquity, it is delicious, easy to prepare, and a classic combination with spaghetti. Grating the Parmesan and Romano cheeses in the food processor or blender cuts down on preparation time.*

**PREP TIME:** 10 MINUTES
**COOKING TIME:** 10 MINUTES FOR SPAGHETTI
**SERVES:** 4

2 generous cups fresh basil leaves, rinsed and
  dried
¼ pound Parmesan cheese, grated
1 ounce Romano cheese, grated
2 medium garlic cloves, or to taste
1 ounce pine nuts
¼ cup good-quality olive oil
2 ounces ricotta or cream cheese
Salt
1 pound dried spaghetti, cooked according to
  package directions

1. Place the basil in the container of a food processor or blender and pulse until coarsely chopped. Add the Parmesan and Romano cheeses, the garlic, and the pine nuts and process the mixture until a paste forms.

2. With the motor running, slowly pour the olive oil in a thin stream into the basil mixture. Blend in the ricotta or cream cheese and add salt to taste.

3. Serve over hot cooked spaghetti, letting each diner toss his own portion.

## SPAGHETTI WITH WALNUT SAUCE

**PREP TIME:** 15 MINUTES
**COOKING TIME:** 10 MINUTES FOR SPAGHETTI
**SERVES:** 4

1 small garlic clove
⅓ cup walnuts
¼ cup olive oil
1 tablespoon walnut oil
½ cup ricotta cheese
½ cup fresh breadcrumbs
4 tablespoons grated Parmesan cheese
¾ teaspoon salt
¼ teaspoon white pepper
Grated nutmeg
1 pound dried spaghetti, cooked according to
    package directions
Fresh marjoram or chopped fresh parsley, for
    garnish

1. Place the garlic and walnuts in the container of a blender or food processor. Pulse until finely chopped. With the motor running, add the olive and walnut oils in a thin, steady stream until mixture is smooth and combined.

2. Blend in the ricotta, breadcrumbs, Parmesan, salt, pepper, and nutmeg to taste. Combine with cooked spaghetti and garnish with fresh marjoram or chopped parsley, if desired.

# SPAGHETTI WITH CHICKEN IN BBQ SAUCE

*Where would we be without convenience foods—canned vegetables of every sort, canned fish, prepared sauces, and condiments? Following are a few recipe ideas using some of these products. Feel free to experiment with other combinations.*

**PREP TIME:** 5 MINUTES
**COOKING TIME:** 20 MINUTES
**SERVES:** 4

2 cups barbecue sauce
4 boneless, skinless chicken breast halves
    (1½ pounds), thinly sliced
1 cup canned white beans
1 (15-ounce) can yellow corn kernels
1 pound dried spaghetti, cooked according to
    package directions

1. Heat the barbecue sauce in a 2- or 3-quart casserole over medium heat. Add the chicken pieces and stir to prevent them from sticking together. Simmer the chicken, covered, over low heat until cooked through, approximately 15 minutes.

2. Add the beans and corn and stir until heated through and thoroughly combined. Serve over the cooked spaghetti.

## SPAGHETTI WITH ITALIAN ANTIPASTO SALAD

**PREP TIME:** 10 MINUTES
**COOKING TIME:** 10 MINUTES FOR SPAGHETTI
**SERVES:** 4

1 (6- or 7-ounce) jar marinated artichoke
    hearts in oil, undrained
1 (4-ounce) jar pimientos, drained and thinly
    sliced
1 cup diced salami
1 cup diced provolone cheese
8 peperoncini
1 teaspoon EACH dried basil and oregano
Freshly ground black pepper
1 pound dried spaghetti, cooked according to
    package directions

1. In a serving dish large enough to hold the
cooked spaghetti, combine the artichokes,
pimientos, salami, cheese, peperoncini, and herbs.
Season with black pepper to taste.

2. Drain the cooked spaghetti and refresh briefly
with cold water. Toss with the salad and serve at
room temperature.

## SPAGHETTI WITH CHICK-PEAS AND FETA

**PREP TIME:** 10 MINUTES
**COOKING TIME:** 10 MINUTES FOR SPAGHETTI
**SERVES:** 4

¾ pound fresh tomatoes, coarsely chopped
2 scallions, thinly sliced
1 cup canned chick-peas, drained
¼ pound feta cheese, crumbled
½ tablespoon freshly squeezed lemon juice
3 tablespoons olive oil
2 tablespoons niçoise olives
2 teaspoons fresh oregano
Salt and freshly ground black pepper
1 pound dried spaghetti, cooked according to
    package directions

1. Toss together the first 8 ingredients in a large
serving dish. Season with salt and pepper to taste.

2. Drain the cooked spaghetti and refresh briefly
with cold water. Toss with the tomato mixture and
serve immediately.

(continued on next page)

## VARIATIONS

CHICK-PEA AND TUNA: Omit the feta cheese. Add to the tomato mixture 1 (7-ounce) can tuna, drained.

TUNA NIÇOISE: Omit the feta cheese from the basic recipe. Add 1 cup cut-up cooked green beans, 1 (7-ounce) can tuna, drained, and 4 anchovy fillets, cut up. Top with 2 hard-cooked eggs, sliced. Serves 6.

## SPAGHETTI WITH WHITE AND BLACK BEAN SALAD

**PREP TIME:** 10 MINUTES
**COOKING TIME:** 10 MINUTES
**SERVES:** 4

**1 cup canned navy beans, drained**
**1 cup canned black beans, drained**
**1 celery stalk, minced**
**1 cup chopped fresh tomato**
**¼ cup minced red onion**
**¼ cup olive oil**
**2 tablespoons minced fresh basil**
**Salt and freshly ground black pepper**
**1 pound dried spaghetti, cooked according to package directions**

1. Combine the first 7 ingredients in a large bowl. Season with salt and pepper to taste.

2. Drain the cooked spaghetti and refresh with cold water. Top with the bean mixture and serve immediately.

# INDEX

Turkey
in chocolate mole sauce, 37
meatballs
spaghetti with, 100
veal and, sage-flavored, 48
in mole sauce, spaghetti with, 36
in Russian spaghetti salad, 115
tetrazzini, 35
Turnip, yellow (rutabaga), in spaghetti with winter
vegetables, 21

## V

Valhalla, spaghetti, 85
Veal
in meatballs Stroganoff over spaghetti, 90
and peppers, 53
in port wine sauce, spaghetti with, 54
and spinach, spaghetti with, 55
and turkey meatballs, sage-flavored, 48
Vegetable(s)
lo mein, spaghetti with, 79
mixed, in orange butter sauce, spaghetti with, 16
Moroccan lamb sausage and, spaghetti with, 52
"pot pie," spaghetti with chicken and, 31
in second wind shrimp and veggie pasta, 97
shrimp with, in coconut milk,
with spaghetti, 77
summer
cottage cheese and, spaghetti with, 109
medley, spaghetti with, 17
winter, spaghetti with, 21

Vegetarian chili, spaghetti with, 18
VELVEETA®
in Mexican-style cheese sauce, 85
sauce with hot dogs, spaghetti in, 85
in spaghetti Valhalla, 85
in tuna noodle casserole, 85

## W

Walnut(s)
blue cheese and, spaghetti with, 108
sauce, spaghetti with, 119
Water chestnuts and mushrooms with pork, with
spaghetti, 74
White bean(s)
and black bean salad, spaghetti with, 122
broccoli rabe and, spaghetti with, 12
White clam sauce, spaghetti with, 58
Wild mushrooms, spaghetti with, 19
Winter vegetables, spaghetti with, 21
Woodsman's sauce, 6

## Z

Zucchini
in celebration spaghetti, 98
in layered marinara bake, 95
and leek, spaghetti with, 22